Frontis Here is a photograph showing congestion in Regent's Canal Dock, London, in the 1930s with massed ranks of coal and timber lighters. These are square sterned craft, similar in design to the Brentford-based dumb barges on the lower Grand Junction Canal, but open holded for non-perishable cargoes. They are delivering coal to the power stations along the Regent's Canal. In the background is the General Steam Navigation Company's steamer *Petrel* on the Continental trade.

E. Paget-Tomlinson

Britain's Canal & River Craft

Moorland Publishing

British Library Cataloguing in Publication Data

Paget-Tomlinson, Edward William
  Britain's canal and river craft.
  1. Inland waterway vessels - Great Britain
  I. Title
  386'.22'0941   VM396

  ISBN 0-903485-90-7

To
Tony Lewery
Who has given so much encouragement

ISBN 0 903485 90 7

Typeset by Alacrity Phototypesetters,
Banwell Castle, Weston-super-Mare, Avon
and printed in Great Britain
by Redwood Burn Ltd, Trowbridge & Esher
for Moorland Publishing Co Ltd,
PO Box 2, Ashbourne, Derbyshire, DE6 1DZ

Contents

Line drawings by the author

Acknowledgements

This has been a pleasant book to write, pleasant because of the great help received from so many individuals. The photographs are credited below, but I would like to emphasize my thanks to museums and libraries staff who have gone out of their way to search out the pictures I required. In particular I would like to record my appreciation of the work of Richard Hutchings, lately curator of the Waterways Museum, Stoke Bruerne, and of Miss Diana Winterbotham of Lancashire County Libraries at Preston. Four photographers have been especially helpful: Kenneth Berry Studios of Hull; Gordon Gledhill of Hull; Barry Munkert of Kingsley, Cheshire, and Real Photographs Company Ltd, of Broadstairs.

Many individuals have placed their photographic collections and knowledge at my disposal; I would specially like to thank Dan McDonald; Commander J. E. G. McKee, Royal Navy; Robert Malster; John Marriage; Andy Millward; Peter Norton; J. G. Parkinson; Don Sattin; Peter L. Smith; Michael Ware; Philip Watkinson; John H. Whitaker (Holdings) Ltd; Mr & Mrs D. G. Wood, Society for Spritsail Barge Research; Reginald Wood.

Above all I must thank Charles Hadfield for his knowledgeable guidance, Mrs J. Stockdale of the Express Typewriting & Duplicating Service of Liverpool, Mrs Ann Sweeney and Mrs Jennifer Snell who had to contend with poor handwriting and difficult technical words. They always triumph.

Source of photographs: Enoch Appleton: 171; Harry Arnold: 93; Barge and Canal Development Association: 68, 90; *Bolton Evening News*: 92; John H. Boyes: 2; Cadbury Ltd: 44; Derek Chaplin: 22; Dr Dennis Chapman: 110; Cheshire County Council, County Record Office, W. J. Yarwood & Sons Ltd records DDX 289: 47, 95, 97, 120, 147; Chiswick Library (Turner Collection): 6; Captain T. E. Claxton: 62; Leslie Cooke: 107; T. P. Crossley: 155; John Dalton: 135; Richard J. Dean: 178; Deegan Photo Co Ltd, Dublin: 134; Stewart Roper Dixon: 4; Dublin Civic Museum and Old Dublin Society: 159; Dudley Public Libraries: 30; Clive Durley: 175; Falkirk Public Library (Telfer Drummond Collection): 123; Graham E. Farr: 13, 15, 16, 20; A. H. Faulkner Collection (J. W. Bell): 53; Captain John Frank: 69, 158; Frith Collection: 38; R. Frost: 79; Guildford Museum: 7; Arthur Guinness Son & Co (Dublin) Ltd: 136; *Halifax Courier*: 66; W. E. R. Hallgarth: 161; Hargreaves Group Ltd: 154; Hertfordshire County Record Office: 140; H. O. Hill collection, National Maritime Museum, Greenwich; 10, 26, 70; Kenneth A. Hitch: 55; James Hollingshead: 34, 144; Hull Incorporated Chamber of Commerce and Shipping: 78; Humber Keel and Sloop Preservation Society: 64, 87; Islington Libraries: 32; W. Jack: 145; City of Kingston-upon-Hull Museums: 71, 77; Lancashire Libraries, Lancaster: 157; Brian Latham: 151; George Lawson: 88, 100; W. E. Leathwood: 105; Leeds City Libraries: 139; Lincolnshire Library Service: 18, 43, 63, 67, 80, 160; R. W. Malster: 56, 58-9, 125; Manchester Central Library: 27; Manchester Ship Canal Co: 111; Robert May: 31; Dr W. A. McCutcheon: 130, 131; Dan McDonald: 124, 126-8, 163, 179; Merseyside County Museums: 33, 112, (*Liverpool Daily Post* Collection): 96, (British Waterways Board Collection): 117; J. E. Metcalfe: 98; Mrs M. Millard: 143; Mitchell Library, Glasgow: 164; George Morrison: 132; National Library of Ireland: 133, 166, 167; National Museum of Wales Schools Service: 21; National Railway Museum: 149; Newark District Council Museum: 72-3; North Yorkshire County Library: 76; Peter A. Norton: 83, 119, 122, 142, 176; P. J. Oke, H. O. Hill collection, National Maritime Museum, Greenwich: 14, 19, 25; J. G. Parkinson: 28, 42, 91, 180; Priestman Brothers Ltd: 172-4; Propellants, Explosives and Rocket Motor Establishment, (Waltham Abbey): 3; Rochdale Canal Co: 65, 102; Rose's of Runcorn: 36, 103; Runcorn Library: 104, 137; Local Studies Department, Shropshire Libraries: 12, 169, 170; Peter L. Smith: 74, 81-2, 84-6, 138, 152; Leslie Speller: 35; H. F. Starkey Collection: 109; John Stevenson: 50-1; River Stour Trust: 60; Suffolk Library Service (Jarman Collection): 57; J. Horace Taylor: 48, 108, 118, 121, 148; Valentines of Dundee Ltd: 75; Valentines of Dundee collection, National Maritime Museum, Greenwich: 9; L. R. Vidler: 11; Waterways Museum, Stoke Bruerne: *frontis*, 5, 8, 46, 49, 54, 141, 146, 162, 177, 181; Waterways Museum and Mrs C. A. Furness: 150; George Watkins: 94; W. Wells: 99; Welsh Folk Museum: 24; Robert Wilson: 52; H. E. Wilton: 61; Reginald Wood: 101;

Illustrations not otherwise acknowledged are from the author's collection.

Introduction

This is a pictorial study of the evolution of river and canal craft in Great Britain and Ireland, arranged in families, the treatment of which is more or less geographical. Families of craft are logical; the waterways centred on the Thames employed craft of similar design and construction, keels were predominant in Yorkshire and so on. Narrow boats admittedly proliferated all over the place, although their home was the Midlands, and some classes of craft have no regional boundaries, passenger packets, tugs, maintenance boats and so on. The families are categorised as follows: The Thames, Severn, Narrow Boats, East Anglia, Yorkshire, Leeds & Liverpool Canal, North Western, Scotland, Ireland, Tugs, Boats in Trains, Passenger Packets, Ferries and Maintenance Craft.

Running through these families are the broad divisions applicable to all canal and river craft. There are two craft categories, if readers will accept a sweeping generalization — they are barges and boats; barges for river work, decked and larger (usually) than canal 'boats', the latter are open holded with no deck or only a small one. However a host of more definitive terms were applied to both categories. Families arose because of the separation of the principal river systems, and thus craft within each system developed their own characteristics of hull design, rigging, sails, oars etc. These were influenced by shoals, currents and the tidal behaviour of estuaries which usually demanded strongly built hulls.

Early river craft of most areas were quite open, with protective cloths over the cargo. The majority carried sails, although they had to rely on haulage from the bank against the current if the wind was foul. Bank traction was by manpower in the early days, and only in the eighteenth and nineteenth centuries were river towing paths provided for horses.

On the River Thames cargo was carried in the early days by open undecked square sailed craft, while the sixteenth-century Severn trow was open, as was the seventeenth-century upriver flat on the River Mersey. Decked craft finally appeared on the Mersey, certainly by the eighteenth century, when the mileage of navigable river was increased by large scale improvements. Vessels on the Humber were probably decked from an early date because of the exposed conditions in the estuary and these keels went up the new Aire and Calder Navigation to Leeds and Wakefield. Decks not only allowed a more weather-tight hull, but gave the crew space for a cabin below. Craft were modernised in other ways during the eighteenth century. Sail design was advanced from the simple square rig to the fore and aft rig which allowed greater use of adverse winds, although many barges kept their square sails, notably Humber keels, which used them very effectively, and some Severn trows. Hull form was influenced by navigation improvement, and limitations of lock chambers forced builders to create shapes which would carry the greatest payload within the prescribed limits.

As river navigations extended, craft grew in number and variety, but they kept their regional features, influenced by local conditions, which is how the families of craft developed. The River Severn (which was actually not improved until the 1840s) had its own style of trows and associated barges, with larger ones for the tidal reaches and smaller ones for the traffic to Shrewsbury and further upriver. The Yorkshire waterways were worked by the great keel family which traded up the Trent, the Witham, the ancient Fossdyke Canal to Lincoln, the Don, the Hull, the Aire and Calder, and the Calder and Hebble Navigations. The Thames system embraced the Wey, the Lee, and via the early nineteenth-century Wey and Arun Junction Canal, the canal line to Portsmouth. In East Anglia narrow, shallow rivers and drainage cuts forced barge operators to couple small craft together in gangs to carry a worthwhile load, while the Broads waterways demanded sailing craft independent of bank haulage, because of the expanse of water and the lack of towpaths. Navigable Scottish rivers were mostly tidal and the Clyde gabbart was as much an estuary as a river craft. In Ireland, Shannon vessels were confined to the river until the canal age, while the Newry Navigation was used by sailing 'gabbards', weatherly enough to cross the expanse of Lough Neagh.

Adaptability was the hallmark of a river barge: keels had to go down the Humber to Hull to load and tranship; flats from the Douglas Navigation had to bring Wigan coal round from the Ribble to the Mersey estuary, and trows depended on Bristol for their cargoes, which meant navigating the Severn shoals with the chance of taking the ground.

Artificial canals extended the range and influence of the river barge families, for canals were designed either to carry a river navigation further inland or to join two navigations across a watershed. Canals were made to suit river craft, for example the Duke of Bridgewater's canal from Manchester to Runcorn had to take Mersey flats, using the rival Mersey and Irwell Navigation, while the long line of the Leeds and Liverpool Canal was intended to allow Yorkshire keels onto Merseyside, as also was the Rochdale Canal. The Kennet and Avon Canal brought Severn trows onto the Thames and Thames 'western' barges onto the River Avon.

The canals, however, did create their own type of craft, many of which were confined to their own still waters. Thus the Leeds and Liverpool Canal, designed for keels, actually had its own type of pure canal boat, unsuitable for river and estuary work because it was open holded. The largest class of craft designed for canal use was the narrow boat, admittedly capable of river and even tidal work in the hands of experienced men like the Gloucester boatmen on the River Severn, but really a still-water type. The choice of such craft to handle the traffic of the Midlands between the Mersey, Trent, Severn and Thames (the Grand Junction Canal was built broad, but because of the tunnels barges were discouraged) is curious, for in this case the canals did not handle the river craft as one would have expected, and indeed as they should have done. Possibly they were built narrow to save money, for their small size did indeed save water. Possibly the choice of a 7ft-wide-lock for the pioneer Trent and Mersey Canal was a decision of the Duke of Bridgewater and the engineers James Brindley and John Gilbert to ensure that the traffic between the Staffordshire Potteries and Liverpool was handled by the Duke's craft on the Mersey, thus forcing the unseaworthy narrow boats to tranship at Runcorn or Preston Brook. A barge line all the way to Stoke-on-Trent would have allowed the potters to carry to Liverpool in their own vessels, to the lasting damage of the Duke.

Narrow boats probably evolved from the simple Worsley mine craft which went underground to the coal face. They grew into a large family with regional variety: Potteries boats; Severners (which were in fact both river and canal craft); Chesterfield Canal boats which sailed on the Trent; Black Country day boats; short narrow boats for the locks on the Calder and Hebble Navigation; and boats for specialist traffic: perishables, tar, sulphuric acid and boxed (containerized) cargoes of coal or limestone.

Akin to narrow boats, but not so narrow, were the canal craft of South Wales, which worked down the valleys from the mines and furnaces to the Bristol Channel ports. Their canals were independent of the rivers whose valleys they used, except on the lower reaches, where for example boats entered the Tennant Canal from the River Neath.

Outside any regional boundary were the passenger packets, the tugs, the maintenance craft, and the method of working boats in gangs or trains, closely coupled together. Passenger packet design was similar on many waterways and the Scottish swift boat was widely introduced in Scotland, Ireland and England. Maintenance boat design depended on the duties required of the craft, ice-breakers were ice-breakers irrespective of where they worked, although some canals did have their own style, for example the Leeds and Liverpool Canal ones of triangular cross-section, and the curious spoon-shaped steam vessel on the Crinan Canal. Tugs were widely introduced during the nineteenth century, particularly on the rivers. They followed all sorts of designs, dependent on their duties rather than on any regional influence, for they were often built miles away from their place of work: Severn tugs at Gainsborough, and Bridgewater Canal tugs at Stony Stratford in Buckinghamshire.

Boats in trains are of particular interest, for this was, and indeed is, a method of passing large cargoes through restricting water channels. The very small canals of East Shropshire and South-West England used tub-boats, floating boxes which could make up a train behind a single horse. The train could be broken up to pass each unit up and down the inclined planes used on these canals, where changes of level were considerable and water short. Push-towed compartment boats on the Aire and Calder Canal are a modern derivative, the compartments nowadays being very large, but able to be handled bodily by the unloading gear at Ferrybridge Power Station. The modern accent is on push towing which gives great control over the train, since the tug is at the back, in the right place for steering and for stopping, and there is no need for any crew aboard the units.

Design of River and Canal Craft

Cargo craft, both boats and barges, were shaped to carry the maximum load possible within the depth of the navigation and the dimensions imposed by locks, tunnels and bridge holes. Passenger boats were planned for speed and comfort and maintenance craft for the work they had to do, such as dredging, ice-breaking and spoil carrying. A great deal of ingenuity went into design, and shallow navigations demanded more thought than deep ones. Upper Severn trows had to be wide in beam with a well-rounded bilge to carry a good cargo over the shallows, while Norfolk wherries adopted a bowl-like cross section with a vee-shaped bottom which would give an improved sailing performance to windward. There was a difference between the lines of a Bridgewater Canal flat, bluff and vertical sided, working on a deep canal, and those of one from the Rochdale Canal, built for a canal becoming progressively shallower. The Rochdale Canal flat was given more rounded sides and a more shapely bow and stern, reducing her cross-sectional area, or in other words the space she would occupy in the water, enabling her to travel or swim better in a confined channel when laden.

Cost and ease of construction were other design considerations. Craft with a flat bottom and square bilge were simpler and cheaper to build than those with a flat bottom and rounded bilge which demanded complex curved frames. Thames sailing barges retained the flat bottom and square bilge and in the early days had the additional simplification of swim ends like a punt. Severn trows had a flat bottom with no central projecting keel, for they were expected to go aground and any projection rendered the hull liable to stick in a sandbank and fail to lift with the tide. Trows could however employ a movable keel, like the 'slipping' keel of a Norfolk wherry. Narrow boats were built with a square bilge and the bottom planking was normally laid crossways. Day boats on the Birmingham Canal system were vertical sided throughout with wedge-shaped ends having no flare, and were very simple to make as no frames had to be shaped.

Weaver flats had square sterns which, besides being easier to make, gave a hull of maximum capacity within the size of the navigation's locks. Square sterns were popular on the Leeds and Liverpool, the Bridgewater, and the Aire and Calder Navigations for the coal barges. Rounded and pointed sterns gave a better flow of water to the rudder of a laden boat and horse-drawn long-distance narrow boats always had a finely pointed stern. Rudders were large, since sharp turns were common on almost all navigations, and they were made long at their bottom edge so that they had plenty of effect if the boat was light. Fore end or bow design received less consideration since the bow had less influence on manoeuvrability. A Yorkshire keel was given a very bluff bow but a fine run aft, but some narrow boats had a remarkably sharp entry. Shropshire Union fly-boats presented a low raking stem with hollow lines, and the Anderton Company boats on the Trent and Mersey Canal achieved a clipper-like grace, a finely-shaped fore end merging into rounded sides, designed for stability with their light but bulky cargoes of pottery crates. The boats would roll, but swiftly return to the vertical.

Boatbuilding

Timber was the universal material for inland navigation craft until John Wilkinson launched the *Trial* on the Severn in 1787. She was an iron barge, designed to carry big loads on a shallow draught. Iron, however, in spite of its versatility, caught on slowly except in Scotland, where iron mineral-scows were introduced on the Forth and Clyde Canal in the 1820s. One reason was that most boatbuilders could not afford the equipment needed to work iron. Wooden boatbuilding lingered on canals and rivers into the mid-twentieth century long after it had been given up for sea-going cargo vessels. But there were compromises; iron bolts and nails replaced wooden trenails, iron knees replaced wood and many craft were iron framed and wooden planked, for example steam barges or packets on the River Weaver. Narrow boats carried this composite construction a stage further when they were built with iron sides and elm bottoms, the latter easily replaced.

Iron was of value for passenger-boat building because it was lighter than timber without sacrifice of strength. The Scots were the passenger boat experts and in 1830 William Houston introduced his first swift boat on the Paisley Canal. Other swift boats started on the Forth and Clyde Canal, the Union Canal, the Grand Canal in Ireland and on several English waterways, notably the Bridgewater and the Lancaster Canals. They were slender craft, shaped like a rowing eight. Cabin sides and roof were built of the lightest possible materials, varnished cotton in some cases, spread over thin ribs.

Iron was also popular for maintenance craft, particularly for ice-breakers, and the Ashby Canal had an iron ice-breaker as early as 1808. This popularity is not surprising, for wooden ice-breakers had to be iron sheathed anyway. Iron was useful for spoil boats which had to take a lot of punishment, as wooden boats quickly strained their planking when loads were carelessly dumped by the dredgers.

Although wooden boatbuilding lingered, many more inland craft were built of iron and later steel, ordered from yards which were established for building estuary and sea-going vessels, coasters, trawlers and tugs. Yarwood's at Northwich on the River Weaver built a wide variety of iron and steel canal craft, as well as Liverpool tugs and African river craft. However some Thames and Medway yards remained faithful to wood between the two World Wars and wooden narrow boats were being built in the 1950s.

One disadvantage of a wooden hull was its poor resistance to the vibration of a diesel engine, and by World War II the diesel was supreme on the inland waterways.

Haulage and Propulsion

River craft depended initially on gangs of men bow-hauling from the bank, struggling along a rough path trodden out by themselves, but bisected by boundary hedges, cut by streams and drainage ditches and hindered by trees and bushes. Horses demanded a properly made gravelled path with gates, which most river navigations achieved by the end of the eighteenth and early nineteenth centuries, except in East Anglia, where stiles had to be jumped and the horses ferried across when the path changed sides. Canals started life with a continuous, unimpeded towpath, interrupted only by tunnels, and horses became established on almost all of them — almost because men were employed still on the Stroudwater Navigation until a horse path was opened in 1827.

Barges were hauled by heavy horses, Shires or Clydesdales, narrow boats by cobs. Mules and donkeys were also used, the latter in pairs. Haulage methods varied, some craft were towed from one of the timber heads on the fore deck, others from a mast set about a quarter of the way aft from the stem, at the point where the hull pivoted when the helm was put over, so that the steering would be less affected by the pull from the bank. Many masts were adjustable in height, which was particularly useful on winding rivers where a high mast would stop the necessarily long line from sagging into the water, thus making the work harder for the horse.

Heavily laden barges sometimes needed two horses, while a single horse might handle a pair of loaded narrow boats. Swift passenger boats employed two or three horses in tandem, the last one ridden by a postillion. Ordinarily with a cargo craft, the horseman walked behind the animal, making encouraging noises with the occasional slap on the rump. Whips were rarely used except to crack to give warning at bridge holes. Passenger boats sounded a horn or trumpet and expected other craft to give way. Passing was indeed the problem with horse haulage when there was only one path; one boat had to drop its line under or lift it over the other, so giving way, and bye laws were careful to state which boat this should be, sometimes the unladen gave way to the laden or the uphill to the downhill. Towpaths on each bank of the busy Birmingham Canal Navigations solved these problems.

Steam power came to the canals as early as 1793 because their still waters were ideal for experiment. But canal authorities winced at the damage their wash did to the banks, so at first steam was only regularly employed in tunnels where tugs saved time, ending the legging and shafting of trains of horse boats. Tugs were not used for general canal haulage until the mid-nineteenth century. On rivers, bank damage was not so critical and there was a tug on the River Severn, then unimproved, in 1830; she was found very useful for working upstream. Steam passenger packets had come to the Yorkshire and Lincolnshire rivers much earlier, to the lower Trent in 1814, to the Ouse in 1816, and to the Witham also in 1816.

Steam tugs paid their way better if they carried some cargo, and the steam barge towing other craft was introduced from the 1850s onwards, first on the rivers, later on the canals, notably on the Leeds and Liverpool Canal and on the Forth and Clyde Canal where the first 'puffer' appeared in 1856. Steam locomotive haulage from a track on the bank was popular in Europe, but in Britain this never progressed beyond the experimental stage. Moving cable haulage was tried in Braunston Tunnel and in Morwellham Tunnel on the Tavistock Canal, while fixed cable haulage, whereby a tug picked up and dropped a cable laid in the canal or river bed, was proposed for the Severn and Trent, tried on the Bridgewater Canal and regularly used by the tunnel tugs at Islington on the Regent's Canal and Harecastle on the Trent and Mersey Canal, the latter being electric.

Electric power over longer distances was considered for several large waterways, such as that proposed in 1902 between the Thames and the Medway, and tried on the Wey Navigation and Staffordshire and Worcestershire Canal, but the oil engine triumphed over all, because of its compactness and because, on smaller craft, it did not need the services of an engineman. But its adoption was slow, and there were few before World War I. Cadbury's of Bournville introduced the Bolinder engine to the canals in 1911. However, oil engines became very widespread in the 1920s and '30s, with low compression semi-diesels giving way to high compression full diesels. Gas engines had been tried in the 1900s, but the gas-producing equipment took up a great deal of space.

Engines and screw propellers (paddles were rare save on river passenger packets) demanded new hull forms with sterns shaped to ensure a good flow of water to the propeller. One problem was cavitation when the propeller lost power in a froth of air and water. Total immersion of the blades was essential, achieved in many craft by the overhanging counter stern which pressed the water down over the propeller and kept the air out. Engine rooms altered the layout of accommodation aboard, sending the Leeds and Liverpool Canal boatmen to live forward, while motor power brought a new pattern of boat working to the narrow canals; steam narrow boats had towed butties, exchanged for others at their destination, while horse boats often worked in pairs, but the motor and butty pair was a permanent arrangement.

Some craft kept their sails (Norfolk wherries, Humber keels and sloops, Severn trows, one or two Mersey flats, and Thames spritsail barges) up to and some a little beyond World War II. Tides and currents aided the work of the sailing barge crews, and made possible the skilful manoeuvering of the Thames lighters.

Decoration

Boat decoration is allied with accommodation and the social life of the boat people. Larger craft were usually worked by an all-male crew, but wives were often aboard, and during the nineteenth century, due to economic pressure, narrow boats became dependent on a family for their operation. Women's influence in the narrow boat world inspired the lavish decoration of the small cabins by graining, painted patterns of contrasting colours, roses and castles, so that they became both cosy and interesting to live in. Exterior paintwork could be remarkably gay and complex, notably on the square sterns of Leeds and Liverpool Canal horse boats. Keels and flats, trows and Wey barges were also painted bright colours but had little patterned work, South Wales canal boats used some simple geometric designs, but Scottish and Irish craft bore little decoration.

Accommodation

Decked barges had the benefit of room below decks for living spaces, frequently both fore and aft, although the principal cabin was generally aft, the forward one often a store and full of anchor cable. Undecked craft had the cabin built up as a low superstructure, giving just sufficient headroom inside, the cabin floor being directly above the keelson. Narrow boat cabins were necessarily cramped so as not to sacrifice cargo capacity. The arrangement of the furniture made the best possible use of available space, in which was housed the cross bed, the side bed, the table cupboard, the stove and drying rail above. Barge cabins were equally neat, the sleeping berths being boxed in, the seats with lockers underneath, and the width of the stern taken up with cupboards, called on the Humber keels the buffet (with the 't' sounded).

1 The Thames and Associated Waterways

One of the largest families of river craft was centred on the River Thames, and because of its numerous tributaries, gradually improved for navigation, the Thames influence spread widely, up the Wey Navigation and via the Wey and Arun Junction Canal down to the Arun Navigation and its offshoot the Portsmouth and Arundel Canal. Influence also spread up the Lee Navigation and its tributary the Stort, up the Grand Junction Canal from where it joined the Thames at Brentford, and up the Basingstoke Canal when this was completed to join the Wey at Byfleet. With the opening of the Thames and Severn Canal Thames craft could reach the River Severn and Severn craft the River Thames, so there was some exchange of design influence here, and the completion of the Kennet and Avon Canal gave Thames craft an extra western outlet.

Parent of all Thames family craft was the swim headed upriver western barge dating from the Middle Ages. This was improved in shape by the end of the eighteenth century, being given a rounded bow and a square or transom stern. This transom stern became a hallmark of Thames family craft and was applied to every member, from the great spritsail coasting barge to the humble Brentford lighter. Another feature of most of these craft was the square bilge or hard chine,

as this was described technically. It dated from the earliest barges, built like boxes and had the advantage of simplicity and cheapness of construction.

Because of their estuarine work before the days of steam tugs Thames craft were for the most part rigged and the fore and aft spritsail was the most common plan. This was only developed in the seventeenth century, earlier craft would have been square rigged, and this remained in the upriver western barge until the eighteenth century. Spritsail rig underwent many modifications and improvements, small mizen masts were added, and the large downriver barges stepped topmasts and topsails, plus a bowsprit and a full set of headsails. The smaller barges which traded on the Lee were 'stumpy' rigged, without topmasts and bowsprit, so they only set a single headsail. Craft on the Arun Navigation and the Sussex Ouse sported a sprit mainsail only, often very crudely fashioned and rigged in the simplest possible manner.

Leeboards were used on most of the sailing barges, and they were necessary to give the hulls a grip on the water when working to windward, but the smaller and simpler rigged craft on the Arun and the Ouse did not have them. They were not, in any case, so refined in aerodynamic design as the leeboards of a Humber keel.

1 Upper Thames or 'western' barges were trading up to Oxford by the end of the twelfth century. Many remained primitive, open holded, punt-shaped

craft into the nineteenth century, rigged at first with a squaresail, later with a spritsail, although dependent on man or horse towage above the tideway. During the eighteenth century some were built to a more rounded cross-section but with a flat bottom and angled bilge. By the nineteenth century they were being given a pointed bow and a wide transom stern, like that of a lower Thames spritsail barge. Man or horse towing was from the masthead, and struggling over shallows and against the current, barges usually worked in pairs. Some traded right through to Brimscombe on the Thames and Severn Canal, while small 60ft by 12ft barges brought salt direct from Droitwich to London. Western barges varied in capacity from 40 to 146 tons, but an average hull size was 80ft long by 12ft beam. This one, loading timber and owned by a Henley carrier, looks a little longer. Note her great flat tiller and tiller pin. She is the subject of a water colour by Samuel Phillips Jackson, first exhibited in 1873.

2 Lee Navigation traffic has been continuous since the days of King Alfred, with sailing craft dominant until the end of the nineteenth century. The barges worked out into the Thames and the hull form was akin to that of the Thames spritsail barge, with a flat bottom, square bilge or hard chine and a transom stern. The Lee spritsail rig, however, was a modest affair, like a 'stumpy' barge — as the bargemen called smaller Thames spritsail barges — but often without a mizen. Lee sailing barges of the nineteenth century measured up to 80ft long by 15ft wide and could carry up to 70 tons. They would use leeboards on the tideway when working to windward, but these would have to be left ashore in the navigation. The photograph shows a barge at Ware.

3 Commissioning of Lee Navigation spritsail barge *Lady of the Lea* in 1931. She worked for the Royal Gunpowder Factory, Waltham Abbey, the last of their fleet of sailing barges. The *Lady of the Lea* measures 72ft in length by 13ft beam and could carry about 70 tons.

4 With steam and motor tugs in service, Lee barges all became dumb craft in the twentieth century. Wooden ones continued to be built during the 1930s, and White's yard at Conyer near Sittingbourne built four between 1934 and 1936, named after places on the navigation, *Enfield, Rye, Leyton* and *Latton*. This view of the frames of one of the four barges shows the square bilge or hard chine very clearly, rounding into the stern which retains the characteristic transom of so many craft of the Thames and her tributaries. These dumb barges were 80ft 9in long and came in two breadths, of 13ft and 15ft. Their laden draught was 3ft 6in, which would mean an 80-ton-capacity for the 15ft-beam barges.

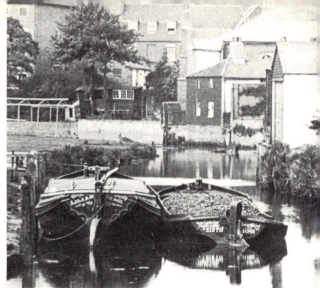

5 Local traffic on the Regent's Canal and on the lower Grand Junction Canal was mostly handled by dumb barges and lighters, the lighters generally swim headed, that is with a punt-shaped bow and stern, the barges with a narrow transom and a very large rudder. These barges would measure 70ft in length by 13ft 6in beam with an under-deck cabin aft. Hatch boards and cloths were fitted to many of them, but these are open holded for the coal trade. They are turning off the Regent's into the Cumberland Market branch near Regent's Park. Horses, tugs and small tractors on the towpath (introduced in 1953) shared the haulage work.

6 Two of the large fleet of barges which worked off the Thames up the lower Grand Junction Canal and the Regent's Canal. One of them, *Edith*, is open holded while the other, *Lilian*, has hatch boards. *Edith* was owned by the Hope Lighterage Company Ltd, of Brentford. The boats are below Brentford gauging lock.

Wey Navigation Barge
One of the last Wey Navigation barges in service, the Hope *belonging to William Stevens and Sons of Guildford. The folding rudder blade is of particular interest.*

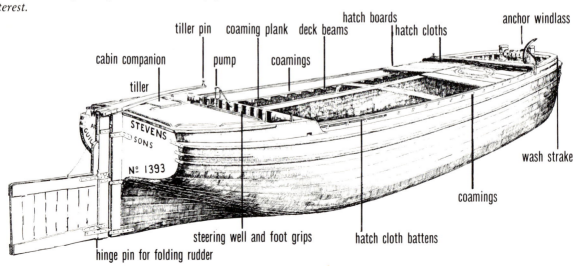

carried an anchor and windlass. They could stow up to 80 tons, the largest measuring 73ft long by 13ft 10in beam. One of the last was *Hope* owned by the Stevens family of Guildford, proprietors of the Wey Navigation. Here she is pictured towing a maintenance boat.

7 The Wey from Godalming and Guildford was an important tributary of the Thames and had its own canal offshoots, the Basingstoke Canal and the Wey and Arun Junction Canal, the latter connecting with the rivers of Sussex and the English Channel. Craft of these waterways bore many similar features and showed a relationship to Thames Western barges, particularly in the shape of the transom stern, the great rudder and the flat tiller with its wooden tiller pin. The rudder was hinged to fold across the stern to fit in the locks. Wey craft, because they navigated the Thames tideway were fitted with low washboards and

8 As it was a broad waterway the Basingstoke Canal saw both barges and narrow boats, the barges being round bilged and transom-sterned like those on the Wey, while the narrow boats had washboards at the fore end. A.J. Harmsworth, at first a carrier then from 1923 owner of the canal, established a repair and building yard at Ash Vale near Aldershot. This is the barge *Aldershot* being built at Ash Vale in 1932, with the boatbuilder using an adze to true up the bevels of the frames. Harmsworth divided his barge fleet into two classes, 'reso's' (residential boats) with living accommodation and 'odd'ns' for day work and lightening other barges, for whereas a Basingstoke barge could carry 80 tons on the Thames, she could only manage 50 tons on the canal, and that only to Woking. *Aldershot* herself measured 73ft 6in long by 13ft 10½in beam, with a 4ft 9in loaded draught. Eventually she became a houseboat on the Wey.

8

9

10

11

9 A sprit-rigged open holded barge on the Arun Navigation above Arundel Castle in the 1900s. She would have a capacity of about 40 tons, measuring some 50ft by 12ft and would have once traded up the Arun Navigation to Pallingham and then onto the Wey and Arun Junction Canal to the Wey and the Thames. Her resemblance to a Wey barge is notable: the transom, the raised stern deck over the cabin and the steering well just forward of the cabin. Other Arun sprit-rigged barges had a pointed stern, while traffic below Arundel was handled by larger craft of up to 100 tons capacity, some lighters working with the tide, while others were sailing barges with hatch boards and coamings, rigged with spritsail, squaresail or lugsail.

10 Barges of 20 to 100 tons capacity were sailed on the tidal reaches of the Sussex Ouse below Lewes, but the 18-ton boats used above Lewes were horse hauled. The locks were tiny, for craft 48ft by 13ft 3in. This is a barge of about 60 tons capacity rigged with a single spritsail. The hold is quite open, but there would be a short deck fore and aft and narrow side decks. Such sailing barges survived into the 1930s, crewed by two who had a simple cabin under the aft deck.

11 Until the 1930s shingle was taken up the Eastern Rother to Rye and above there by small shallow draught sailing barges which also went up the tidal River Brede and up the Royal Military Canal, bow hauled from the bank in the latter instance. The barges were pointed at both ends with short decks fore and aft and an open hold, each deck having a cabin or cuddy under it. The rig was a single standing lugsail and the hulls were flat bottomed, but round bilged and strongly built, to lie aground at low tide in the Rother estuary loading shingle by shovel and wheelbarrow, for which wheeling boards and boxhorses were carried.

17

2 The Severn and the West Country, and South Wales

Severn traffic was dominated by the trow in its various forms, and the trow hull shape was seen in other west country navigations, for example on the Stroudwater Navigation and as far west as Devon, where the Teign clay barge and the Tamar gravel barge formed a kind of cadet branch of the family. Trow features were the square stern and rounded bilge, coupled with a full body and blunt fore end; although upriver trows, because they worked in such shallow water, had to have a carefully worked out hull form in order to carry a decent payload. Their hulls were saucer shaped, as beamy as possible, coupled with a modest freeboard.

In rig, west of England craft followed the pattern of other areas; square sails gave place to fore and aft except on certain navigations where the square sail was quite adequate, as on the Stover Canal near Newton

Abbot and on the upper Severn, where the current was the main means of propulsion. Leeboards were never employed, for trows and their sisters were given a movable keelboard.

Other West Country craft bear no relation to the trow. The little barges on the River Parrett in Somerset seem to have been a race apart, double-ended and open-holded, while the canal craft of South Wales were built on lines similar to the English narrow boat but to different dimensions.

Severn motor craft either followed the Yorkshire style or were built with a dual role in mind, to operate out into the Bristol Channel as far west as Swansea. Thus they looked like, and indeed were, miniature coasters.

12 There were two main members of the trow family (in this instance trow rhymes with 'crow'), the larger working in the Severn estuary and Bristol Channel, the smaller not coming below Gloucester, but going upriver when the depth allowed to Coalbrookdale, Shrewsbury and Pool Quay near Welshpool, the limit of navigation. Upriver trows were open-holded, shallow draughted craft. They were often called frigates or just barges, measuring say 50ft by 15ft and carrying 20 to 40 tons in the eighteenth century, but with a capacity of up to 80 tons in the nineteenth century. Many kept a square

rig to the end, unlike their estuarine cousins. No improvements were made to the River Severn above Stourport and boats depended on floodwater for progress. They might have to be content with a laden draught of less than 3ft, while there were Severn craft, called flats, which loaded 20 tons on a draught of 18in. This photograph of Ironbridge with an upper Severn trow loading dates from about the end of traffic on this part of the river; by 1884 the Coalbrookdale-Bewdley horse path had ceased to take tolls. This trow appears to be square rigged, while the open hold is covered by tarpaulins.

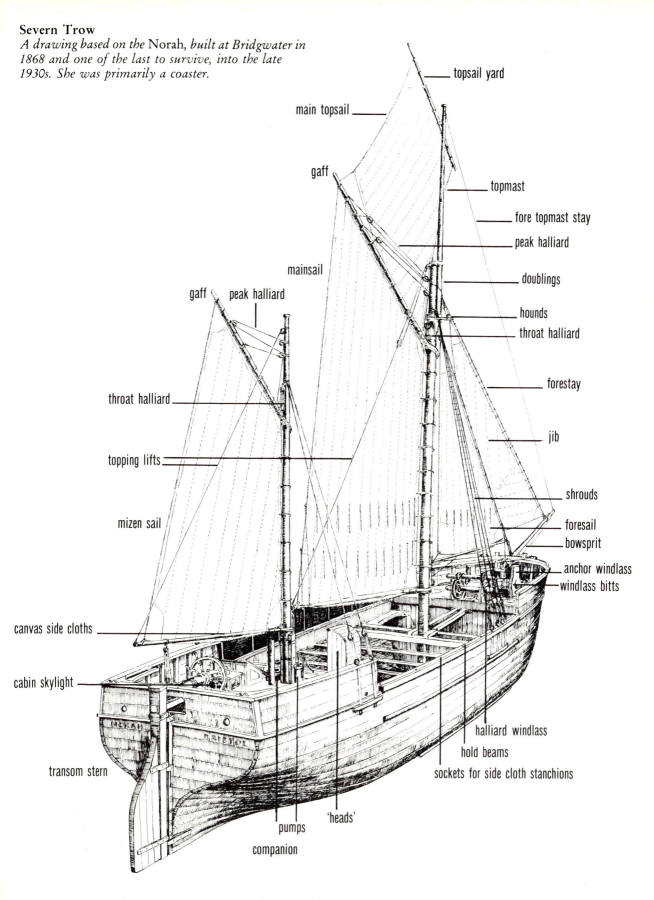

Severn Trow

A drawing based on the Norah, *built at Bridgwater in 1868 and one of the last to survive, into the late 1930s. She was primarily a coaster.*

topsail yard

main topsail

gaff

topmast

fore topmast stay

peak halliard

doublings

hounds

throat halliard

mainsail

forestay

jib

gaff

peak halliard

throat halliard

topping lifts

shrouds

foresail

bowsprit

anchor windlass

windlass bitts

mizen sail

canvas side cloths

cabin skylight

halliard windlass

hold beams

sockets for side cloth stanchions

transom stern

pumps

'heads'

companion

19

13

13 Trows of the lower Severn and its estuary, originally square rigged, were in many cases altered in the nineteenth century to a more weatherly fore and aft smack or ketch rig. This was because, from the 1830s, tugs and barges were taking much of the river traffic, and trows were forced to seek cargoes from the Bristol Channel ports, notably South Wales coal. Nevertheless many sailing trows remained on the Severn, notably the 'Wich barges, in the Droitwich salt trade. Trows were flat bottomed, because they often went aground and almost all of them had a most distinctive deep transom stern, like a 'D' lying on its back. The open hold, protected by canvas side cloths became a danger to the coasting trow and some were given hatches. The ketch trow *Alma*, built in 1854 at Gloucester and named after the Crimea victory, was the last under sail, trading until 1943. In this 1939 picture the rails for extending the side cloths are clearly seen, the vessel being on the gridiron outside the Floating Harbour at Bristol, a form of tidal dry dock which allowed access to her bottom. *Alma* measured originally 69.8ft long by 15.9ft beam by 5.8ft depth of hold, but in 1916 she was rebuilt to 77ft × 17ft × 6.3ft, 58 tons gross register.

14 Stern view of the trow *Alma* in the Cumberland basin, Bristol in 1936. This shows the D-shaped transom stern, and the open hold, protected by the side-cloths.

15 Opened in 1827 the Gloucester and Berkeley Ship Canal remained the deepest and widest canal in England until the Manchester Ship Canal was completed. Designed for 600-ton ships it still is a busy waterway and nowadays can take 1,000-ton capacity oil tankers. During the 1930s the old established Severn and Canal Carrying Company introduced a series of steel motor barges to trade between the Bristol Channel ports as far west as Swansea and the Severn, five being tankers, three for dry cargo. The first of the latter was the 119 gross ton *Severn Trader* built in 1932 by Charles Hill of Bristol, as were all these craft. The photograph, taken in 1950 when the dry cargo fleet was being run by the British Transport Commission, shows her entering Avonmouth.

16 Petroleum traffic to Worcester and Stourport saved the Severn in the later 1920s and remained important until the 1960s. The Severn and Canal Carrying Company had their first motor petroleum barge *Severn Tanker* built in 1935 by Charles Hill of Bristol, followed by four more. Regent Oil and John Harker of Knottingley, Yorkshire were other petrol barge operators, Harker acquiring the Severn and Canal craft in 1948. Here in 1951 *Severn Tanker* approaches the entrance lock to Gloucester docks from the Severn. She could carry 250 tons, her hull measuring 88.2ft by 18.6ft.

17

17 John Harker's *Arkendale H* started life as a dumb barge, being built in 1937 by Richards Iron- works of Lowestoft for the Severn petroleum traffic. She was motorized in 1948, with a capacity for 340 tons of 'black oil' or crude petroleum. She is seen here in Gloucester Docks on her way back to Swansea to re-load on 21 October 1960. A few days later, 25 October, she collided with another Harker tanker in the Severn, the pair of them bringing down two spans of the Severn Railway Bridge above Sharp-

ness. The spans fell across the barges and caused an explosion in which five men lost their lives.

18 Watson's of Gainsborough built motor tugs for the Severn and Canal Carrying Company, for work on the Severn, towing trains of barges and narrow boats. This is *Enterprise*, completed in 1930, and later re-named *Severn Enterprise*. Note the portable rivetting hearth on the cabin top.

18

19 A new type of barge appeared on the Stroud-water Navigation and the Thames and Severn Canal in the 1820s to handle coal from the Forest of Dean. This was an open holded craft called a Stroud barge, built with a flat bottom and a square bilge like a narrow boat, but with a bow somewhat like a trow and with a pointed stern. Stroud barges were about 68ft long by 12ft 6in beam with a capacity of 50 tons of coal. Since they were out in the Severn estuary, coming across from the coal port of Bullo Pill, they were strengthened by a massive keelson and set a single square sail. Some lasted as dumb barges into the 1930s, towed by tugs on the Severn and horse hauled up to Stroud, Brimscombe and Chalford. This is one of the last, *Perseverance*, abandoned on the bank at Ryeford in 1936. The photograph shows a view aft from the mast tabernacle.

20 The short Lydney Canal was opened in 1813 as a ship canal from the Severn estuary up to the town. Coal from the Forest of Dean, the main traffic, was shipped until 1960, but latterly all cargoes were incoming, logs for the plywood mill in steel barges, towed up from Avonmouth. These ones photographed in 1956 were owned by Benjamin Perry of Bristol.

20

Glamorganshire Canal Company Boat

The stem was curved so that the greatest strength came at the loaded water line. They were 60ft long by 8ft 6in beam and could carry 20 tons on a 2ft 9in draught.

stem iron

towing mast

stud and mooring chain

21 Busiest of the South Wales canals was the Glamorganshire Canal, particularly from the 1830s when Rhondda coal began to be intensively mined. Most of the boats were crewed by two men, and wives and families were rare. Cabins were unadorned and because mining subsidence reduced bridge clearances, chimneys were cut down to roof level. The boats were similar to English narrow boats and measured 60ft by 8ft 6in beam, loading to 20 tons of coal on a draught of 2ft 9in. This photograph shows a 1930s scene at Pontypridd, by that time the limit for traffic. The horseman has the horse's nose tin slung on his back.

21

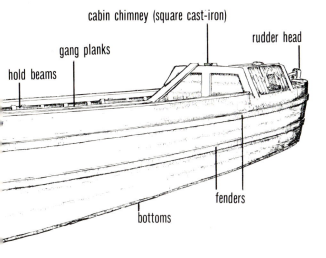

hold beams
gang planks
cabin chimney (square cast-iron)
rudder head
fenders
bottoms

22 Boat weighing machines were built on three British canals to literally weigh boats suspected of carrying more than their waybill stated. They were inverted weighbridges, the one on the Glamorganshire Canal being built by Brown, Lennox and Company at their Pontypridd chainworks in 1836. First at Tongwynlais, it was later moved to various sites in Cardiff, and now rests at the Waterways Museum at Stoke Bruerne. The gable-end shaped plate on the cabin side carried the initials GCC (Glamorganshire Canal Co), the boat's fleet number, in this case 451, the last in use, and her registration number with the local authority under the Canal Boats Acts of 1877 and 1884, whereby craft were classed as dwellings and subject to health inspections.

23 Few South Wales canal boats have survived intact, this one on the Neath Canal at Tonna being destined for preservation. Neath Canal boats were mostly without cabins because trips were short. They measured 60ft by 9ft and could carry 24 tons of coal. Like Birmingham day boats the helm could be hung at either end from the vertical stem and sternposts.

22

23

24

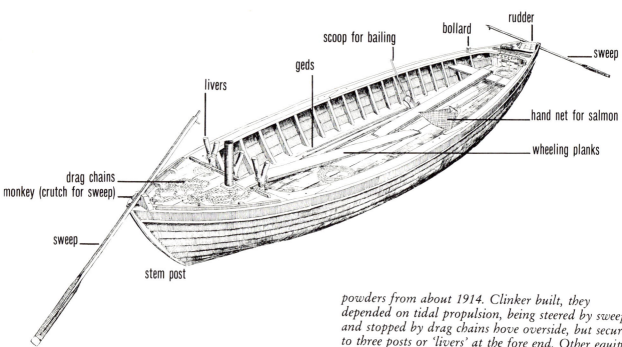

livers

scoop for bailing

geds

bollard

rudder

sweep

hand net for salmon

wheeling planks

drag chains

monkey (crutch for sweep)

sweep

stem post

River Parrett Barge

The River Parrett in Somerset was the main artery of a complex system of navigation which included the River Tone, the Ivelchester and Langport Navigation, the Westport Canal, the Bridgwater and Taunton Canal and the Chard Canal, and it had its own barge family. The larger ones were used in the Parrett estuary to dredge up silt for the Bridgewater bath brick industry, killed by the introduction of cleaning powders from about 1914. Clinker built, they depended on tidal propulsion, being steered by sweeps and stopped by drag chains hove overside, but secured to three posts or 'livers' at the fore end. Other equipment included boathooks or 'geds' for mooring in mud, a bailer, a net for surface swimming salmon and planks for wheeling the silt aboard in barrows. Salmon netting was a lucrative sideline. These estuary barges measured 53ft long by 13ft beam and carried 25 tons of silt. There were smaller ones restricted to the rivers and canals, of 18 tons capacity, and boats called 'shoes', smaller again, 20ft long by 8ft wide, of 5 tons capacity, for canal work only, possibly hauled in trains.

24 'Scholar boating', in other words a school outing, was popular long before the present day pleasure cruising enthusiasm. Actually this is more likely to be a chapel outing, at Gilwern on the Brecknock and Abergavenny Canal in the 1900s. The boat is identical in size and shape to Glamorganshire ones, the same canoe-shaped stem and wedge shaped fore end, the prominent wooden rubbing strakes or fenders along the hull, the lozenge and crescent decoration on the top plank fore and aft. Cabins were universal on the Monmouthshire Canal and the Brecknock and Abergavenny Canal as it was a 42-mile trip from Newport to Brecon.

25 Quarrying of ball clay remains a big industry in South Devon, for which in 1792 the Stover Canal was opened, and much later in about 1843

the shorter Hackney Canal, to carry the clay down to Teignmouth for shipment. Single square sailed barges were used with capacities of up to 25 tons, with square sterned hulls, 50ft long by 14ft beam by 5ft in depth. On the canals they were bow hauled, hoisting sail in the Teign estuary. Latterly, on the Stover Canal a motor tug was used throughout. Each clay company's craft were identified by the colour of their gunwales, white for these Watts, Blake, Bearne & Company barges which lie by the thick walled clay sheds at Teigngrace on the Stover Canal. The barge in the centre is *George V*, the photograph being taken in October 1937, by which time they were all unrigged; traffic ended on the Stover Canal by 1939, on the Hackney Canal in 1928.

26 Brunel's Saltash bridge is the background to this Tamar sailing barge, *Lillie*, built in 1899 and owned by a Saltash man. She carried limestone, coal, grain and timber up to Newbridge near Gunnislake, the head of the Tamar Manure Navigation, so called because the limestone was burnt in riverside kilns and as lime was spread over the fields. The photograph, taken in September 1923, shows the usual square stern of these vessels and the jackyard topsail which the larger ones set. Barges measured some 50ft long by 16ft beam and carried up to 80 tons. There was a crew of two, with a cabin below deck aft.

3   Narrow Boats

In England narrow boats are synonymous with canals, and they have been studied and written up in greater depth than any other craft. A close inspection of British waterways as a whole reveals, however, that in fact they were restricted to the English Midlands, and a greater mileage of waterways was built to broad standard for barges of various types. Certainly narrow boats invaded these broad waterways, some indeed were specially made so that they could use them, for example the Huddersfield Canal boats which could go on the Calder and Hebble Navigation. On the purely narrow waterways narrow boats came in various shapes and sizes for the small variations of lock dimensions that existed, and there were some specialist designs for liquid cargoes (particularly chemicals), for crated pottery and chinaware, for steel tubes, and for perishables, But, apart from the liquid carrying boats, they remained open holded with only canvas cloths for protection.

Historically they seem to have evolved from the little mine boats at Worsley whose boxed coal cargoes were transferred at Worsley basin to craft of similar shape but larger dimensions for the journey to Manchester. Some of these 'box' boats were in use until recent years, unchanged in design for two centuries. The great fleet of Birmingham and Black Country day boats follow a similar hull form with few refinements, but long distance 'cabin' boats were given more shape, particularly if they were fly boats running non stop with relays of horses.

The introduction of steam and diesel power meant some changes in hull design, notably the counter stern, while some narrow boats, for instance those on the Chesterfield Canal working out onto the Trent, actually set a square sail as regular practice. The narrow boat style of design and construction was extended to wider and longer craft on canals whose locks and bridges would take them: the 'wharf' boats on the BCN (Birmingham Canal Navigations), the wide boats on the Grand Junction and the so-called 'bastard' boats on the Bridgewater (bastard because they were the size of a barge but the shape of a narrow boat).

Worsley Mine Boat and Box Boat

Narrow boat evolution: a small Worsley mine boat on the left which worked in the underground system right up to the coal face and on the right a box boat, of full narrow-boat dimensions which carried the coal in boxes with bottom-opening doors. The mine boats varied much in size, from two to ten tons capacity, while the box boats could carry up to twelve 35cwt boxes. This is a 68-footer working on the Manchester, Bolton and Bury Canal with ten boxes.

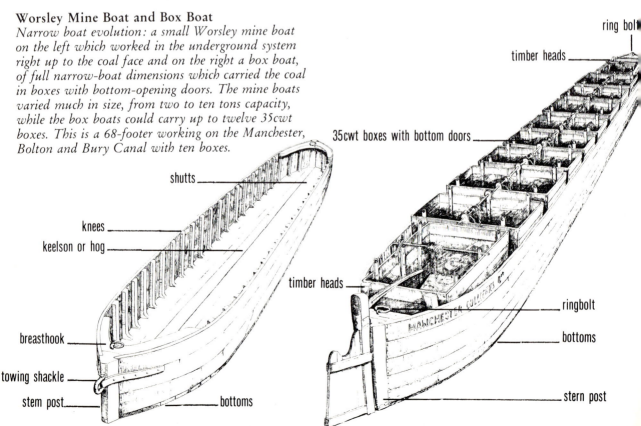

27 Among the earliest canal craft in the British Isles were the Duke of Bridgewater's mine boats at Worsley near Manchester which used the navigable levels made from the 1750s onwards to reach the coal face. They were a simple wedge-shaped design with stout wooden knees and according to a report of 1842 came in three sizes: M (mine) boats of 10 tons capacity, narrow boats of 8 tons, tub-boats of

2 tons. After coal removal by water ceased in 1887 at the time of this illustration, some stayed as maintenance craft, while others were broken up or sunk. This is the wider of the two Worsley mine entrances, for unladen boats going in.

28 Enlarged versions of the mine boats, to the same simple wedge shaped design, were the open narrow coal boats without cabins which worked on the Bridgewater Canal, the Manchester, Bolton and Bury Canal and Fletcher's Canal, a private colliery branch. They were usually only 68ft long because of the locks on the Manchester, Bolton and Bury Canal, and many carried coal in boxes. This was an early idea, attributed to James Brindley, for he designed the waterwheel-powered crane which lifted the boxes from the canal to street level at Castle-fields, the Manchester terminal of the Duke's canal from Worsley. Boxes were used into the 1950s, latterly with iron bottom doors closed by chains passed round a spindle. Capacities ranged from 8 to 35cwt and boats could carry a dozen boxes. This pair are derelict at Astley Green Colliery, Tyldesley.

29 Although photographed in 1971 this narrow boat in the dry dock at Worsley on the Bridgewater Canal could have dated from the 1760s, as the first boats used on the Duke's canal from his Worsley mines to Manchester were of this appearance. There is no attempt to give any shape to the fore end, the planks are simply pulled in to a wedge, and it is the same at the stern. These craft were 68ft narrow boats without cabins and carried coal either loose or in boxes. Latterly they were maintenance craft used by the National Coal Board to deal with subsidence problems in the Tyldesley-Leigh area.

30 Canal traffic on the complex Birmingham Canal Navigations existed in a world of its own, employing vast fleets of narrow 'Joey' boats to serve mines, quarries and ironworks. The principal routes, which extended on three main levels, not only joined up with long distance canals, but pushed out arms to colliery and factory and later to railway goods stations. Journeys were short so the boats were not lived in, except for the odd night. Many were quite open, others had short cabins (box cabin boats) and it was common for the rudder or helm to be transferred from one end to the other to save winding or turning. Such boats were 'double ended' with vertical stem and stern posts, others were 'round stemmed' where the helm could be hung on the stern only. These wooden 'open' boats are loading at Haden Hill Colliery wharf, Old Hill,

near Dudley, in the 1920s. The helm lies in the bottom tilted against a beam, so that it can be shipped easily.

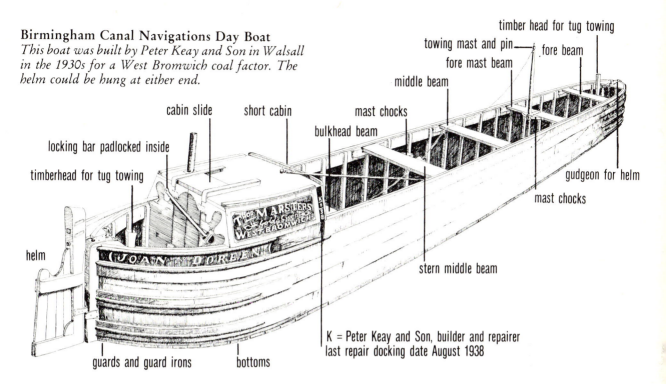

Birmingham Canal Navigations Day Boat
This boat was built by Peter Keay and Son in Walsall in the 1930s for a West Bromwich coal factor. The helm could be hung at either end.

Labels:
- timber head for tug towing
- towing mast and pin
- fore mast beam
- fore beam
- middle beam
- mast chocks
- bulkhead beam
- cabin slide
- short cabin
- locking bar padlocked inside
- timberhead for tug towing
- helm
- guards and guard irons
- bottoms
- stern middle beam
- mast chocks
- gudgeon for helm

JOAN DOREEN

THOS MARSTERS WEST BROMWICH

K = Peter Keay and Son, builder and repairer
last repair docking date August 1938

31 Not all Birmingham and Black Country boats were narrow boats, as some could carry up to 40 tons if the water allowed it. On the lock-free length between Brindley's old main line at Bilston and Tipton and on the Wyrley and Essington Canal from Wolverhampton onto the Cannock Extension Canal and further out to Anglesey Basin, a wider, longer boat was possible, up to 86ft long by 7ft 9in wide, the limiting factor being the turn into the Wyrley and Essington Canal at Horseley Fields Junction. These wharf boats or 'Ampton (Wolverhampton) boats could carry up to 50 tons behind a single horse. This sunken one belonged to E.W. Read, a fuel merchant, and illustrates both the shape of the box cabin and the characteristic day boat cabin end decoration for recognition purposes, since crews delivered one boat and came back with another. The timber head was needed for towing in trains when boats were secured close up, the stem of one overlapping the stern of the next ahead. This was called 'stemming', and it saved steerers.

32

33

32 From E.W. Cooke's *Shipping and Craft* published in 1829 comes this plate of a small stumpy rigged Thames spritsail barge and a pair of narrow boats. E.W. Cooke was an exceptionally accurate marine artist and his proportions are unlikely to be wrong, so the narrow boats then must have been more rounded in hull form with taller cabins. The water cans on the cabin top are similar to today's. This pair have rigged a mast and sail between them to assist progress on the tideway.

33 With the opening of the Grand Junction Canal in 1805 London had a direct canal link with the Midlands and a heavy traffic developed, later fed by the entirely urban Regent's Canal, completed in 1820, which brought canal boats down to the real port of London. The Regent's Canal also provided wharves and basins more central to London, and the great City Road basin, 2½ furlongs in length, became London's canal depot for carriers to the Midlands and the North. Pickfords moved here from Paddington and this engraving by Thomas Shepherd, one of a series showing scenes on the new Regent's Canal executed in 1826-7, illustrates a Pickfords' narrow fly-boat, with the distinctive lozenge on the cabin side. Most of Pickfords' services were fly, in other words night and day using relays of horses, the main traffic being from London to Birmingham and Manchester. Fly boats were initiated on canals and rivers in the 1790s to compete with road services.

34

34 A boat horse at Acton Bridge on the Weaver Navigation in Cheshire. This seems an exceptionally powerful animal. Note the wooden bobbins or spools threaded along the traces to check chafe. The reins ran through rings on the straps to the swingletree, and the whole equipment was liberally decorated with brass studs and plaques.

35 Many boat horses would walk on without driving, although it was usual for the boat captain to be on the bank with them. This is a horse boat called *Lottie*, owned by Cowburn and Cowpar of Manchester, loaded with barrels of chemicals on the Bridgewater Canal near Dunham Park in May 1936. The horse hauls from a short telescopic mast which has a spring loaded pin which will slip the line should the boat overrun the horse and threaten to drag him into the water.

36   Raw materials for the Potteries, china clay, felspar and flints and the return cargo of crated ware from the Five Towns made up much of the Trent and Mersey Canal's traffic. The Anderton Company was long established in the trade, being founded in the early nineteenth century under another name but reconstituted as the Anderton Company in 1836. Their narrow boats, called for some reason 'knobsticks' and built at their Burslem dock, were notably fine lined with rounded sides, to ensure stability when loaded with bulky, but not very heavy crates raising their centre of gravity. They would roll about but return upright. This photograph shows a boat at Runcorn, the port for the Potteries, awaiting a cargo of raw materials, perhaps clay brought from Cornwall by topsail schooner. Behind is the six-storey Alfred dock crate warehouse.

37   Probably a Mersey-Weaver narrow boat leaving Dutton locks on the Weaver Navigation. The horse is well ahead of the picture, towing on a long line as was usual on river navigations, with the horse-man well behind him. The Mersey-Weaver Company was a subsidiary of the Salt Union and ran narrow boats between the Staffordshire Potteries and Anderton in Cheshire where they had transhipment sheds. On the Weaver they had their own flats towed behind Salt Union steam packets, but their narrow boats also worked down to Weston Point.

38   A postcard view of the Shropshire Union Canal's flight of locks at Tyrley, south of Market Drayton. The boat is one of the Thomas Clayton, Oldbury, fleet of gas or oil boats, so called because they carried gas water (for the making of ammonia), tar, creosote and oil, in bulk. The hold was a long narrow tank with intermediate swill boards to check surges of liquid when working through locks. Loading and unloading was done through lids on the deck and the short post at the fore end of this motor boat carried a headlight and served as a guide to the steerer when the boat was empty. With her stem well up seeing ahead was difficult. Thomas Clayton Ltd, founded in 1842, retained their canal fleet until 1966 and several of their craft are preserved in cargo-carrying trim.

MKD.34.F. TYRLEY LOCKS. MARKET DRAYTON.

Anderton Company
Horse-Drawn Wooden Narrow Boat

They were designed with fine lines and a rounded cross section for speed and stability; they carried light yet bulky crates of pottery which raised their centre of gravity, but because of the round hull form they would roll yet remain upright.

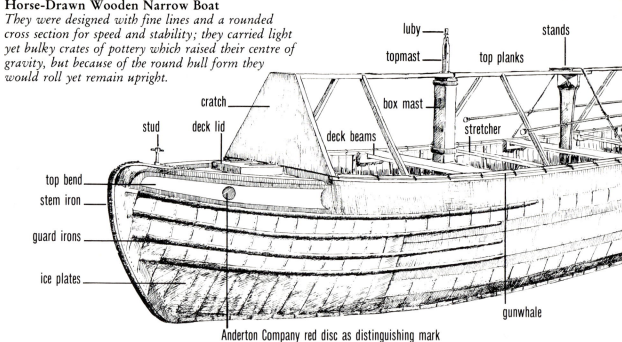

luby
stands
topmast
top planks
box mast
cratch
stretcher
deck lid
deck beams
stud
top bend
stem iron
guard irons
ice plates
gunwhale

Anderton Company red disc as distinguishing mark

39

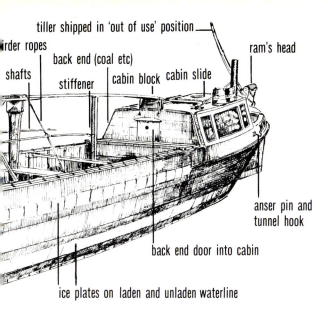

tiller shipped in 'out of use' position

rder ropes

shafts

back end (coal etc)

stiffener

cabin block   cabin slide

ram's head

anser pin and
tunnel hook

back end door into cabin

ice plates on laden and unladen waterline

39 Narrow boats were built with a sharp stern before engines were fitted, and the butties or towed boats retained this traditional shape which allowed easier manoeuvrability. The lines aft were fined down to allow the maximum play of water on the rudder. On both narrow boats and barges the rudder is large: it has to be to act on a long hull; moreover it has to work efficiently whether the boat is empty or laden, so the blade is both broad and deep, This is an empty butty leaving Trentham Lock on the Trent and Mersey Canal in 1959. She is an ex-Birmingham 'station' boat, built for day work between factory and railway goods station, but one of a number made into long distance cabin boats by British Waterways in the 1950s.

40 Genuine family narrow boats were used a good deal in the coal trade on the Bridgewater Canal from the South Lancashire pits to Runcorn and Lymm gasworks, although they would have been too wide for many narrow locks and too deep for many narrow canals. They were built with six or seven planks which would add up to a depth of 4ft 6in or more in the hold, so they could carry 30 tons of coal. Some were engined, being given a counter built round the horse boat stern, the counter being ballasted with concrete to keep the propeller immersed. Jonathan Horsefield was the last Runcorn carrier and these are two of the company's boats near Preston Brook on a wet Sunday in December 1956. Harry Bentley in the preceding motor *Elizabeth* has devised a hutch-like rain shed, and his wife Sarah has rather effectively propped up the slide. Note the stout timber heads for tug work which were a feature of these craft.

40

41 An immaculate pair of Samuel Barlow narrow boats working up the Marsworth flight of locks on the Grand Junction Canal in April 1956. The motor boat (left) is *Malta*, while the butty (right) is *Cylgate*, once a horse boat on the Oxford Canal trading independently as a Number One, owned by the Hone family. The picture clearly shows the difference between a horse boat and motor boat: the motor boat with a counter stern overhanging the propeller and a balanced rudder, the butty with a sharp stern and heavy helm, as the rudder is usually termed. The motor's counter checked cavitation of the propeller by ensuring it was kept immersed. Note too the greater height of the motor boat cabin because of the need for the floor to be above the propeller shaft.

Steel Motor Narrow Boat
No 161 Pinner *built by W.J. Yarwood and Sons Ltd, Northwich, for the Grand Union Canal Carrying Company. She was one of the 'Town' class ordered in 1936 with 4ft 9½ in deep sides, designed to carry cased goods. Building of the steel hulled motor boats was shared between Harland and Wolff of North Woolwich and Yarwood's. Eventually by 1938 186 pairs of boats were completed for the Grand Union Canal Carrying Company.*

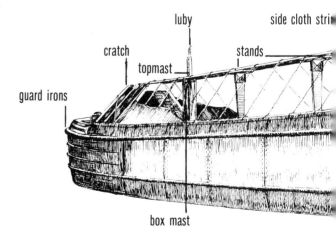

42 A pair of narrow boats belonging to Jonathan Horsefield of Runcorn, crossing the Barton swing aqueduct in August 1956; the motor is *Loretta*, the butty *Marjorie*. Compared with Midlands narrow boats they were rather plain, dark green being the cabin side colour of the Horsefield fleet.

42

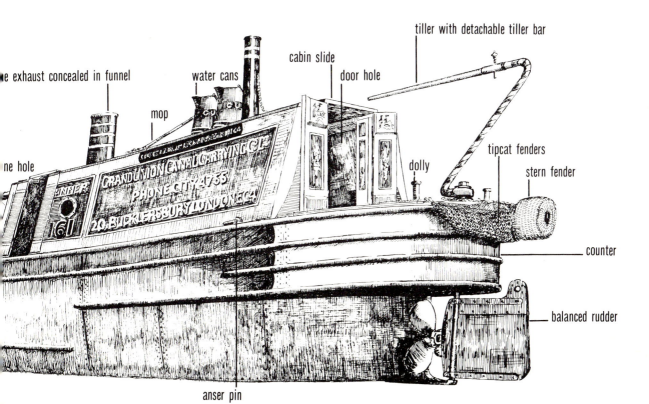

43

43 In this 1900s view of Brayford Pool, Lincoln, where the Witham Navigation and Fossdyke Canal meet, are the expected assembly of keels, rigged with derrick poles for cargo working. In the foreground is the distinctive type of narrow boat which went up the Chesterfield Canal, which was built to narrow dimensions above Retford. These craft had to navigate the River Trent, for which they set a single squaresail like a miniature keel, hence the halliard roller at the stern. Accommodation was under the stern deck.

44 The largest of all narrow boats were the Severners, craft which worked on the River Severn and its associated canals. They measured up to 72ft in length by 7ft 2in beam and could carry as much as 45 tons. The biggest fleet was that of the Severn and Canal Carrying Company Ltd, who had trows, barges and tugs for Severn work, capable of towing long trains of narrow boats. Much of the company's traffic was to Cadbury's at Bournville on the Worcester and Birmingham Canal and this picture dating from the 1930s shows several pairs of boats at Waterside, the Bournville wharf. Many of the motor boats were not named but numbered and could handle two laden butties. They were painted blue

and white, both men and boats being nicknamed 'toe-rags'.

45 On narrow canals new boats were being built of wood as late as the 1950s, the last in 1959 at Braunston, but nowadays even repair facilities for traditional wooden craft are few. One yard which keeps going in the old way is Peter Keay and Son of Walsall who in 1970-1 docked the Thomas Clayton tar boat *Gifford* for the North Western Museum of Inland Navigation. Very extensive replanking was needed at both ends, the tar cargoes having successfully preserved the middle. *Gifford* was built in 1926 at Braunston and is now on show to the public at Ellesmere Port.

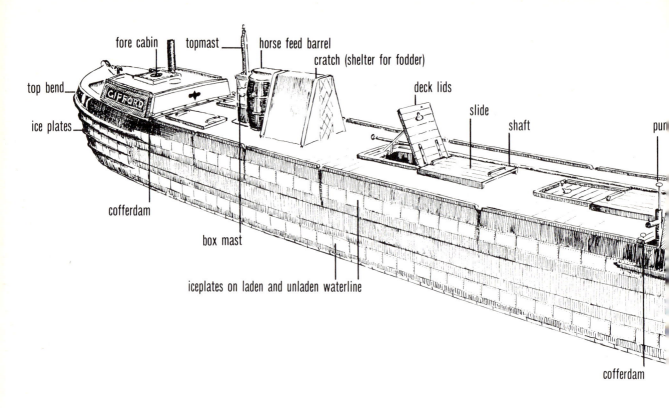

fore cabin · topmast · horse feed barrel

cratch (shelter for fodder)

top bend

GIFFORD

deck lids

slide

shaft

pur

ice plates

cofferdam

box mast

iceplates on laden and unladen waterline

cofferdam

46

PHŒNIX Nº 54

CLAYTON, Ltd

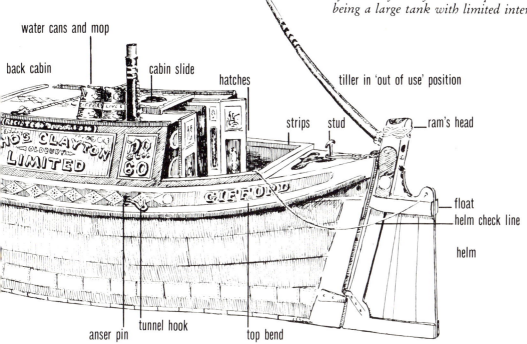

Thomas Clayton Tar Boat
Built by Nurser's of Braunston in 1926 Gifford is the sole restored survivor of a large fleet of horse-drawn wooden narrow boats operated by Thomas Clayton of Oldbury. They carried liquids in bulk, the hull being a large tank with limited internal sub-division.

water cans and mop

back cabin

cabin slide

hatches

tiller in 'out of use' position

strips

stud

ram's head

float

helm check line

helm

anser pin

tunnel hook

top bend

46 By far the largest fleet of steam narrow boats were operated by Fellows, Morton and Clayton as fly-boats trading from Brentford to Braunston, from City Road basin, London, to Birmingham and Coventry, with services also to Leicester, Nottingham and Derby. They were powerful craft, having tandem-compound engines, and they towed one or two butties, but they could only carry 12 or 13 tons themselves, hence the need to keep them continually on the move to earn their living. This view of *Phoenix* shows the whistle and safety-valve escape pipe, also the box which seems to have been a cover for the engine hole skylight. The two ladies are unlikely to be part of the steamer crew, probably coming from the butties.

47 Many narrow boats were built with iron or steel sides and cross boarded elm bottoms, like this one for Fellows, Morton and Clayton at Yarwood's, Northwich in the 1930s. The freshly-sawn bottoms can just be seen, the boat being fully equipped and ready for launching. Composite construction started in the 1890s, and was popular because when bottoms wore out they could easily be replaced. Some boats had the lowest side strake made from wood too.

47

Steam Narrow Boat

Fellows, Morton and Clayton steam narrow boat
Marquis with an iron composite hull built at Saltley,
Birmingham, in 1898. Converted to a motor boat in
1925.

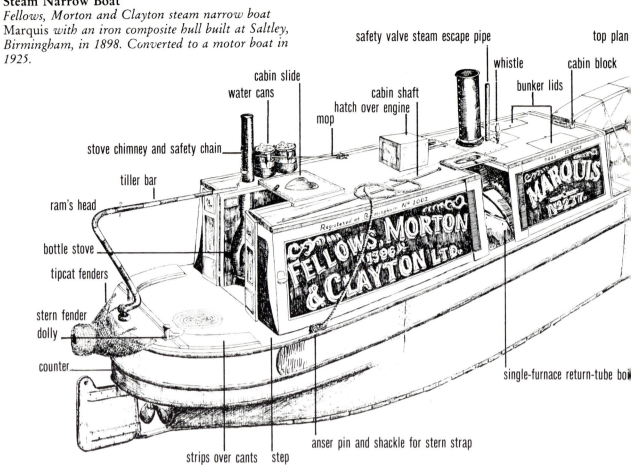

safety valve steam escape pipe

top plan

whistle

cabin block

bunker lids

cabin slide

cabin shaft

water cans

hatch over engine

mop

stove chimney and safety chain

tiller bar

ram's head

bottle stove

tipcat fenders

stern fender

dolly

counter

single-furnace return-tube boi

strips over cants   step

anser pin and shackle for stern strap

48

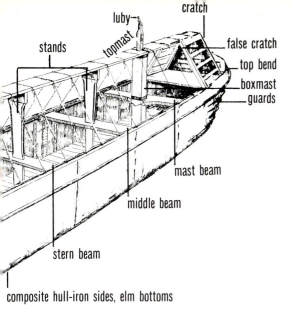

stands
luby
topmast
cratch
false cratch
top bend
boxmast
guards
mast beam
middle beam
stern beam

composite hull-iron sides, elm bottoms

48 Steam cargo-carrying narrow boats were numerous in the 1900s, but were quickly eclipsed by diesel powered boats in the 1920s. However one latter day steamer was *Sentinel* built in 1927 by J.H. Taylor and Sons of Chester for C. Payne Crofts of Northampton. She had a Sentinel steam-lorry boiler and engine, although this was removed fairly soon in favour of a motor because of difficulties of ash disposal. *Sentinel* is seen here at Taylor's Chester yard.

49 Wide boats were much used in the sand and gravel trade on the lower part of the Grand Junction Canal from as far out as Leighton Buzzard to the London wharves. H. Sabey and Company Ltd of Paddington were well known carriers and this is their *Southwold* at Marylebone. Wide boats were built like narrow boats, to the same length but 10 or 11ft wide on the gunwale, the bottom width being 7ft only, for the sides were rounded in to lessen water resistance. Because of their cargo these gravel boats were not clothed up, but those carrying grain and merchandise had the normal narrow boat's side and top cloths.

49

50 The layout of a narrow boat cabin was a masterpiece of ingenuity, and the arrangement of furniture never altered from what had become a traditional pattern. The stove was always on the left with a brass drying rail above, flanked on its right-hand side by the table cupboard, whose door fell outwards to become the table. The main bed ran across the back of the cabin from side to side, but a child could sleep on the side bed facing the stove. This picture of part of the cabin of the ex-Grand Union Canal Carrying Company's butty boat *Argo* shows the amazing wealth of decoration to create interest and give a feeling of more space in a cabin of less than 10ft by 6ft 10in. Brass bed knobs, lace-edged plates and crotchet work were universal, while the chain of wartime army haversack clips was a spare for the chimney, to hold it in case it fell off under a bridge or low bough.

51 Another view in the cabin of the narrow boat *Argo* with the black-leaded stove, the brass drying rail, a painted dipper and plenty of lace-edged plates, one from Blackpool and another showing a transporter bridge, possibly Runcorn, but more likely Newport, Monmouthshire.

52 Canal narrow boat decoration has come in for much comment and speculation as to its origin, but the truth is fairly simple. Originally they were dull craft when crewed by men only, but when in the early nineteenth century women came aboard with

their families, they became floating homes. Few women would put up with the spartan accommodation as it existed and set about brightening up their cabins with ornamental brasswork, gay chinaware, embroidery, and painted patterns and pictures, copied one suspects from contemporary cottage furniture, decorated crockery and long case clock dials. Most of this work was restricted to inside the cabin, as canal carrying companies were not so enthusiastic on expensive exterior decoration. It was applied however by the owner boatman and by some companies, notably by the Samuel Barlow Coal Company whose work was taken over in 1962 by Blue Line Cruisers of Braunston. This is their *Raymond* in Buckby locks in 1970, the last year of the regular coal run to London. The 'cratch' supporting the forward end of the gang planks is red with a lozenge pattern in red, blue, yellow and white and two flower paintings.

4 East Anglian Craft

East Anglia has a wide variety of waterways, from the Ancholme Navigation in the north to the Chelmer Navigation in Essex. It includes the Norfolk rivers and the broads and the complex Fenland systems. The craft used were equally varied and do not make up a local family like the Thames barges and their sisters. In Lincolnshire Humber keels and sloops worked up the Ancholme, the Louth Navigation, the Fossdyke Canal and the Witham Navigation, for these waterways are offshoots of the Humber, but the River Nene and the Fens waterways were dominated by the small local lighters, working in trains or gangs of four or five behind a single horse. This method gave them great flexibility of operation in the narrow channels and tight corners of the system. There were larger craft on the Ouse and the Cam, either tug towed or self propelled, but their size limited them to the principal rivers. Very similar to the Fens lighters were those on

the River Stour in Suffolk which worked in gangs of two behind a single horse. They were of the same hull form and were steered in the same way, the second lighter being fitted with a long steering pole which turned the whole boat into a vast rudder.

Broadland bred its own distinctive sailing craft, working independently of bank towage as they had to cross open water. The square rigged keel, which had no affinity with the Humber keel, gave way to the extremely manoeuvrable wherry, with her huge black gaff mainsail. Wherry hulls were well designed, as they had to carry a worthwhile cargo in shallow water. Indeed shallowness was the obstacle to East Anglian navigation. The Chelmer Navigation would only admit a laden draught of 2ft, and the River Gipping in Suffolk 3ft, so the barges were built as beamy as possible.

53

53 Lighters in the Alexandra Dock, King's Lynn, before World War I. Those in the foreground belong to the Lee family of Stanground near Peterborough, and they are from left to right: *Rosedale*, *I Don't Know How It's Done* and *The Return*. Dutch influence seems apparent in the rounded

stem, the pronounced sheer and the wide clinker planking, but the scroll work on the top plank looks a local touch. Like Norfolk wherries, Fens lighters also had white painted quadrants or 'nosings' either side of the stempost.

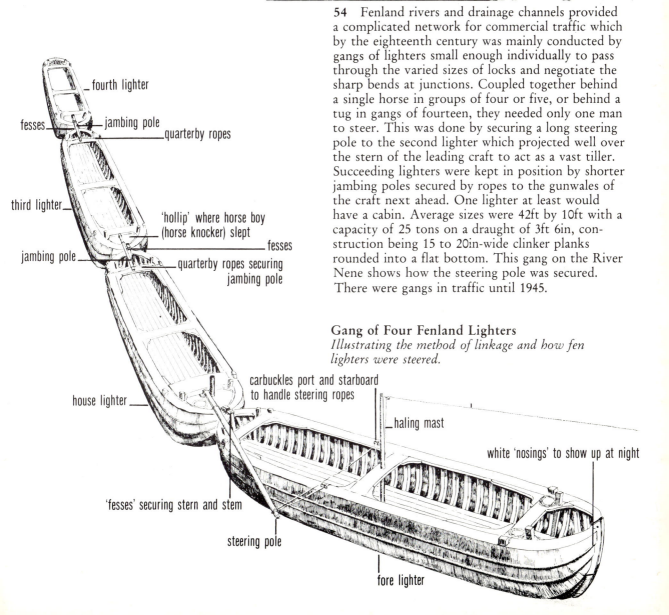

54 Fenland rivers and drainage channels provided a complicated network for commercial traffic which by the eighteenth century was mainly conducted by gangs of lighters small enough individually to pass through the varied sizes of locks and negotiate the sharp bends at junctions. Coupled together behind a single horse in groups of four or five, or behind a tug in gangs of fourteen, they needed only one man to steer. This was done by securing a long steering pole to the second lighter which projected well over the stern of the leading craft to act as a vast tiller. Succeeding lighters were kept in position by shorter jambing poles secured by ropes to the gunwales of the craft next ahead. One lighter at least would have a cabin. Average sizes were 42ft by 10ft with a capacity of 25 tons on a draught of 3ft 6in, construction being 15 to 20in-wide clinker planks rounded into a flat bottom. This gang on the River Nene shows how the steering pole was secured. There were gangs in traffic until 1945.

Gang of Four Fenland Lighters
Illustrating the method of linkage and how fen lighters were steered.

fourth lighter

fesses

jambing pole

quarterby ropes

third lighter

'hollip' where horse boy
(horse knocker) slept

fesses

jambing pole

quarterby ropes securing
jambing pole

house lighter

carbuckles port and starboard
to handle steering ropes

haling mast

white 'nosings' to show up at night

'fesses' securing stern and stem

steering pole

fore lighter

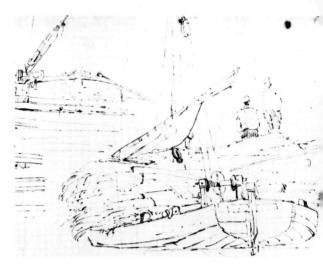

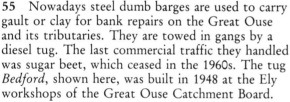

55 Nowadays steel dumb barges are used to carry gault or clay for bank repairs on the Great Ouse and its tributaries. They are towed in gangs by a diesel tug. The last commercial traffic they handled was sugar beet, which ceased in the 1960s. The tug *Bedford*, shown here, was built in 1948 at the Ely workshops of the Great Ouse Catchment Board.

56 Norfolk keels working inland from Yarmouth to Norwich, Beccles and up the Bure, were the forerunners of the well known wherry which superseded the older craft during the eighteenth century. The keel, of medieval descent, had a single square sail, a long hatch apparently without covers and a wide, round bilged, vee bottomed hull which was

the pattern followed by the wherry. This shape enabled a good cargo to be carried in and on a hull which drew little water, a necessity in the shallow rivers and broads. Accommodation was forward in a raised cabin, for a crew which could number four, since these vessels became larger to compete with the wherry. The largest was the *Success* of 1795, 97-tons burthen, although 30 tons had been an average keel capacity for a craft measuring 54ft 6in by 14ft 6in. This is a detail from a series of ink drawings of keels at various angles, from an unknown source; the design of stern and rudder was carried over to the wherry.

57 The River Lark is a tributary of the Great Ouse up to Mildenhall and Bury St Edmunds, but navigation had decayed by the mid nineteenth century. It was briefly revived in the 1890s by the Eastern Navigation and Transport Company Ltd, when they restored the navigation up to a mile short of Bury and introduced steam tugs; this is No 3, built on narrow boat lines, as were other Fenland tugs widely introduced towards the end of the nineteenth century. They had water ballast tanks to keep the propeller immersed. Some of the lighters in this picture have hatches. Traffic to Bury St Edmunds ceased after 1894 when a receiver was appointed to the moribund company.

57

Norfolk Wherry

Wherries enjoyed their greatest prosperity during the nineteenth century before railway competition became too severe. Their hulls, almost all clinker-built, were designed to carry a good payload, of around 25 tons, on a draught of some 4ft when the freeboard amidships would be nil. Moreover they were so shaped, with their hollow bow, to work well to windward, aided by the mast being stepped so far forward and by the high peak of the great black gaff sail, the only sail they carried. This was hoisted by a single halliard whose task was made possible by an arrangement of blocks and chain spens to distribute the load. The mast could lower for bridges. Note the 'nosings' at the bow to show her up at night. Length 52ft, beam 14ft.

martingale

chain spens

gaff line

'high' vane

herring hole

gaff

mainsail

trolleys

3 rows reef points

tapered halliard

forestay

windlass barrel swings aside to allow mast heel to rise

bonnet

horsa

forestay blocks

carling board

bin iron

harpens – overhang of covering board fore and aft

0-fathom dropping hain for controlling peed when shooting idges

24ft quant

coburg

interlocking hatch boards

shifting right ups

nosings

plankways

standing right ups

plancea

slipping keel

timber heads

mast tabernacle

clinker planking

dead hatch

58

59

58 Some sailing wherries were unrigged and converted to power, like this one towing a reed barge on the River Thurne in 1959. The reed barges, small craft which were quanted (shafted) into the great reed beds, gathered reeds for thatching and marsh hay for cattle. In this instance the little barge is used as a lightening boat for the wherry to partly unload her cargo in shallow waterways.

59 A few so-called steam wherries were built, including the 65-ton capacity *Opal*, built at Gainsborough in 1896. She had a steel hull which, with its counter, did not look at all like a wherry's, although the white 'nosings' were there. *Opal* was first owned by John Crisp and Sons, the Beccles maltsters who had another, *Topaz*. Latterly *Opal* was operated by the Great Yarmouth Shipping Company and in this 1950s scene is alongside the spritsail barge *Cambria* at Norwich. *Opal* had a small compound engine and generally towed one or two lighters, each carrying 80 or 90 tons.

60 Locks on the Suffolk Stour could pass a couple of lighters in one operation, and it was usual for these craft to be permanently linked in pairs, each measuring about 46ft in length by 10ft 6in beam, with a loaded draught of 2ft 5in which allowed a cargo of 13 tons per boat. The lighters were clinker-built with wide planks rounding into a flat bottom, and were decked, with the hold protected by coamings and hatch covers. Steering was achieved by using the second boat as a rudder controlled by a 30ft-long steering pole secured to her fore end and passing over the stern of the leading lighter to a steering well between the two hatches. The horse was always ridden and had to jump the stiles across the path. Two horses were sometimes needed to go upstream, while on the tidal part of the river lighters were sailed or poled, the sail being a crude square one.

61 Fertilizers were the last cargoes on the River Gipping, or Ipswich and Stowmarket Navigation, and were carried until 1930. Both Messrs Fison's and Packard's had several steam barges which towed two dumb craft apiece. Like the barges on the Chelmer Navigation these were also shallow draughted, 3ft only, the locks allowing a maximum length of 55ft and a maximum breadth of 14ft. 30 tons was as much as each craft could carry, the steamers less because of their machinery, situated aft. This is the Packard's steamer *Mersey* (they were named after rivers) approaching the fertilizer works at Bramford four miles above Ipswich.

5 Yorkshire and Trent Craft

Yorkshire keels are historic craft which dictated the size of locks on the river navigations, all of which were improved with keels in mind. Connecting waterways like the Barnsley Canal and the Dearne and Dove were built to keel standard, and the Leeds and Liverpool Canal was intended as a keel waterway, although keels did not normally use it. The keel family was quite complicated, the word keel actually referring to the square rig and not the hull, while the word sloop meant a similar hull with a fore and aft rig. Hull sizes varied and some so-called keels did not set sails at all, being purely inland craft, which rarely if ever ventured on the Humber estuary. In fact there were accepted divisions into tidal and non tidal keels, the latter often open holded. Non tidal craft could also be called 'boats', the best known being the West Country 'boats' working down from the Calder and Hebble Navigation whose locks limited their length to 57ft 6in. West Country boats would rarely use leeboards or set a sail.

Keels worked up the Trent, although there was a Trent variety called a 'catch', some of which stepped a lug-rigged mizen mast. The varieties of Trent craft are complex, some dumb, some sailing, the latter including the smaller open holded upper Trent boats, which were in fact keels with a square sail but rarely leeboards. At the other end of the keel scale was the coasting billyboy, either single masted or ketch rigged, and the similar 'dickie', while the family embraced the Aire and Calder Navigation's fly-boats, hauled by horse on the navigation, and towed by tug down to Hull.

Steam power allowed extensive towage services to be introduced in Yorkshire, some of the tugs becoming cargo carriers and called steam keels. Motor barges, generally called river craft, followed the keel shape, indeed many were once sailing keels. Purpose built ones were given an unkeel-like counter stern, and they continue to be built for the oil and gravel traffic.

62 The Rainbow Bridge at Conisbrough, upstream from Doncaster was opened in 1849 and carried the South Yorkshire Railway (from 1864 part of the Manchester, Sheffield and Lincolnshire Railway) over the River Don. From 1889 the Don was incorporated in the Sheffield and South Yorkshire Navigation. This keel is an old clinker-built one, clinker or over-lapping planking being replaced by carvel or flush planking during the nineteenth century. Pit props coming from Scandinavia via Hull or Goole form a high deck load, the horse hauling from a tall 'neddy' or post stepped in place of the mast. The date must be about 1910.

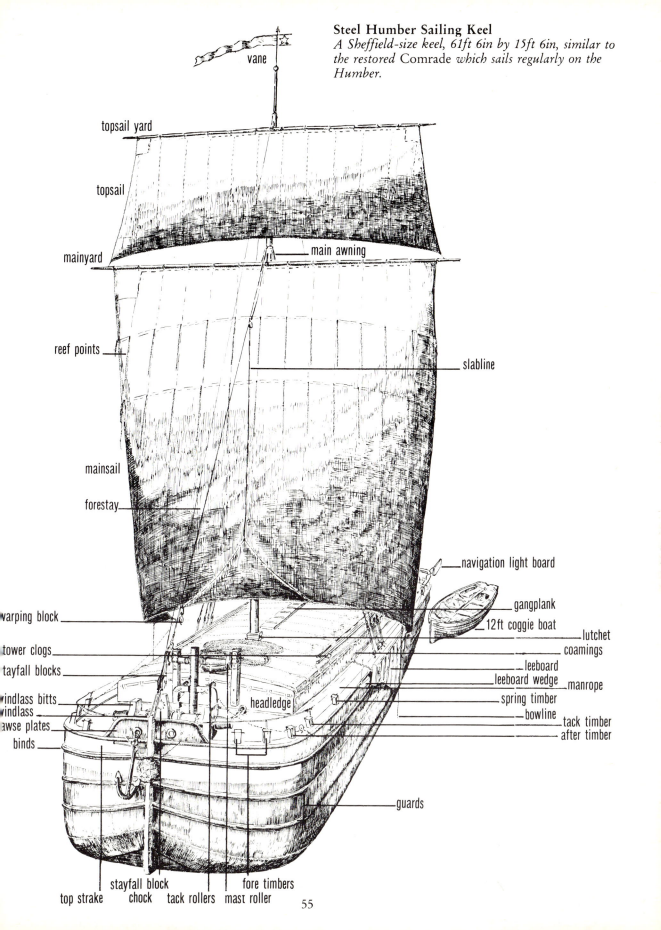

Steel Humber Sailing Keel

A Sheffield-size keel, 61ft 6in by 15ft 6in, similar to the restored Comrade *which sails regularly on the Humber.*

vane

topsail yard

topsail

mainyard

main awning

reef points

slabline

mainsail

forestay

navigation light board

gangplank

12ft coggie boat

lutchet

warping block

tower clogs

coamings

tayfall blocks

leeboard

leeboard wedge

manrope

windlass bitts

spring timber

windlass

headledge

bowline

tack timber

hawse plates

after timber

binds

guards

top strake

stayfall block

chock

tack rollers

fore timbers

mast roller

55

63

63 Yorkshire waterways, which are almost all river navigations, have had an uninterrupted history of commercial activity since they were first improved in the early eighteenth century. The prime navigation is the Aire and Calder, from Goole to Leeds and Wakefield. Most of the traffic until the advent of motor craft was handled by keels, sailed on the Humber but horse hauled on the rivers and canals. They were square rigged with mainsail and topsail (and very occasionally a topgallant sail), and being flat bottomed with only a shallow external keel they used leeboards for working to windward. Sizes varied, depending on where a keel traded: Lincoln size, 74ft 9in by 15ft; Manvers size (trading to Manvers Main colliery on the Dearne and Dove Canal), 58ft by 14ft 10in; Driffield size, 61ft by 14ft 6in; and most common of all the Sheffield size, 61ft 6in by 15ft 6in, for the River Don or what became after 1889 the Sheffield and South Yorkshire Navigation. Capacities ranged from 60 to 80 tons. Many keels of the nineteenth and twentieth century were built of iron and later steel. This is the steel *Loxley* built in 1925 at Thorne and owned by Furley's of Hull, on the Trent. Note the cog or coggie boat for running lines and general work, lying astern. A steel keel, *Comrade*, is preserved in sailing condition by the Humber Keel and Sloop Preservation Society.

64 Bow hauling was the rule on the earlier river navigations before paths were laid for horses, and it was continued to recent times by Yorkshire keels to save the cost of hiring a horse. This couple, Mr and Mrs Bill Dean, are helping their keel, *Danum*, along the Sheffield and South Yorkshire Navigation by 'bow yanking' as they called it, for which both wear a canvas harness or 'seal.'

65 Many keels were less deep in the hold than those working up from the Humber, 6ft 6in as opposed to the 7ft 6in of the Humber keel. Some of these shallower 'Yorkshire' keels went up the Calder and Hebble Navigation whose upper locks limited them to a length of 57ft 6in and a breadth of 14ft 2in. Calder and Hebble craft were called 'West Country' boats, because they came from the extreme west of the West Riding, their size also enabling them to go over the Rochdale Canal to Manchester and then via the Bridgewater Canal and Leeds and Liverpool Canal to Liverpool. This vessel, *Emily*, is actually one of the Rochdale Canal Company's own carrying fleet at Mirfield, a great boatbuilding centre on the Calder and Hebble Navigation. These keels, with coamings and hatch-boards, could and did go on the Humber, either under sail or behind a tug.

64

65

66

67

66 One of the last wooden 'West Country' boats to be built was the motor *Bradsylda*, launched at Mirfield on 25 January 1954 for the Bradford Dyers' Association Ltd. Here she is at Ganny lock, Brighouse in June 1955, with a load of coal for the dyeworks at Brighouse.

67 Towards the end of the nineteenth century the Trent Navigation Company built up a carrying fleet of sailing keels and dumb craft, the iron and steel dumb ones being called 'pans'. There were horse hauled 72ft by 14ft open holded iron Nottingham pans for work above the city to Burton (via the Trent and Mersey Canal), Leicester and Grantham. After the river improvements of the 1920s, the steel Trent pans, decked with hatches, were 82ft 6in by 14ft 6in wide by 5ft 3in depth of hold, loading to 100 tons on a 5ft draught. They were towed between Hull and the Trentside wharves up to Nottingham by the tugs of the United Towing Company of Hull, whose *Riverman* is here seen at Keadby alongside two keels, *Brasso* and *Samaritan*. *Riverman* was built in Holland in 1915; *Brasso* in 1924 and owned by Reckitt and Colman, makers of

the metal polish of the same name; *Samaritan,* ex-*Nile* of the Trent Navigation Company, in 1883. In the background are three pans under tow and a steam keel towing two keels which have set small sails to help.

68 Sloops were the fore and aft rigged sisters of keels, with the same shape of hull, built to the same series of dimensions, but with a gaff mainsail, a foresail and sometimes a jib extended by a bowsprit. Whereas keels were mostly owned in Yorkshire, Hull, Goole, Thorne and Stainforth sloops came in the main from the Lincolnshire side of the Humber — Barton, New Holland, South Ferriby. They traded to the same places but made more coastal passages than a keel. Here a sloop rounds the end of the Corporation Pier to enter the Old Harbour at Hull in 1936. With the captain at the helm, the mate at the halliard rollers prepares to lower the mainsail.

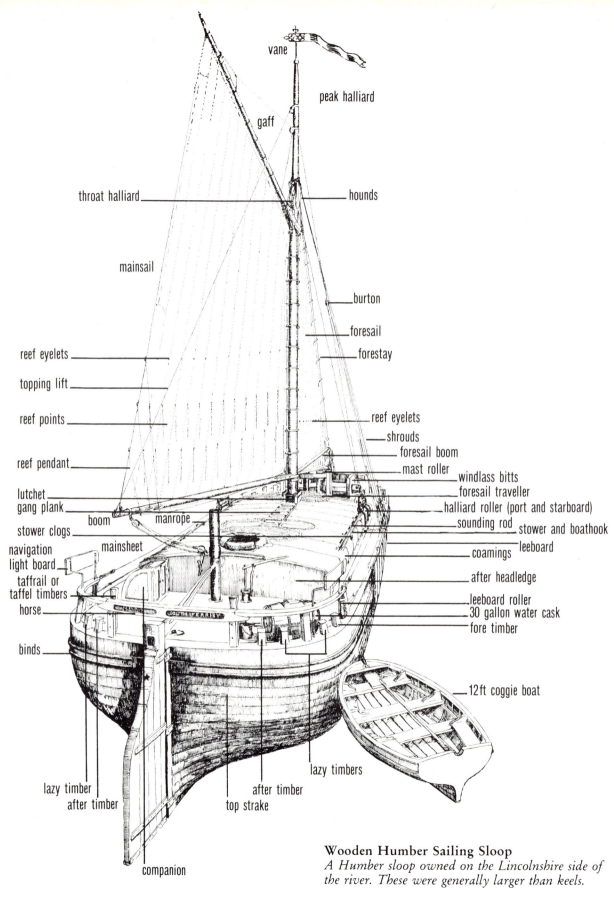

vane

peak halliard

gaff

throat halliard

hounds

mainsail

burton

foresail

forestay

reef eyelets

topping lift

reef points

reef eyelets

shrouds

foresail boom

reef pendant

mast roller

windlass bitts

foresail traveller

lutchet

halliard roller (port and starboard)

gang plank

sounding rod

stower and boathook

boom

manrope

stower clogs

leeboard

mainsheet

coamings

navigation
light board

after headledge

taffrail or
taffel timbers

leeboard roller

horse

30 gallon water cask

fore timber

binds

12ft coggie boat

lazy timbers

lazy timber

after timber

after timber

top strake

companion

Wooden Humber Sailing Sloop
*A Humber sloop owned on the Lincolnshire side of
the river. These were generally larger than keels.*

69

69 Unloading coal from the sloop *John and Anne* at Ferriby Sluice, at the mouth of the Ancholme Navigation in the Humber Estuary. A derrick pole is rigged to whip the baskets out of the hold. Note the halliard rollers on the hatch coaming.

70 A third member of the keel family was the billyboy, which had a hull like a keel's, although with more sheer. She used leeboards, but because she was a coaster, some having capacities of 100 tons, she had bulwarks and could be either cutter-, ketch- or schooner-rigged. This is an early photograph of a cutter-rigged billyboy with square topsails, the *HH* of Goole, taken at Shoreham, at the mouth of the River Adur in Sussex, in February 1864. The topsail schooner alongside, to the right

of the picture, is the *Elizabeth* of Bridgwater. Billyboys were clinker-built, as were keels in the nineteenth century, and some were still trading up and down the East Coast until the end of World War I.

70

71 Trent 'catches' (ketches) had a sharper stem than a keel and measured 74ft by 14ft or shorter. They worked up from Hull to Lincoln and Nottingham. This is a small model of the *Brothers* of Hull, built in 1887, which made regular coastal passages. Catches had a wider foot to the mainsail than a keel to give more power, for the hull was longer than a keel's. The leeboards show prominently in the model, and were designed to give the hull a grip on the water when working to windward. Note also the lugsail on the mizen, a feature of some catches, hence the allusion to the ketch rig.

72 Cargoes on the Trent above Nottingham, on the Nottingham Canal, on the Soar to Leicester, on the Grantham Canal and on the Trent and Mersey Canal to Burton were handled by Upper Trent boats, which could be described as miniature keels of 40 to 50 ton capacity, 60ft by 14ft, open holded, with a single squaresail and sometimes leeboards, all of which gear was put ashore before going up the Soar and the Nottingham and Grantham Canals because of the low bridges. Although horse hauled on the Soar and the canals they were sailed on the Trent, often, as here, setting their sails when under tow behind one of the Trent Navigation Company's tugs. In this case (although not in the picture) she is the *Little John*, Trent Company tugs being named after Robin Hood and his followers, as indeed they still are.

72

Upper Trent Boat

*One of the fleet of boats owned by the Trent Naviga-
tion Company, rigged like a keel, but open holded
with canvas covers, and in this case no leeboards.*

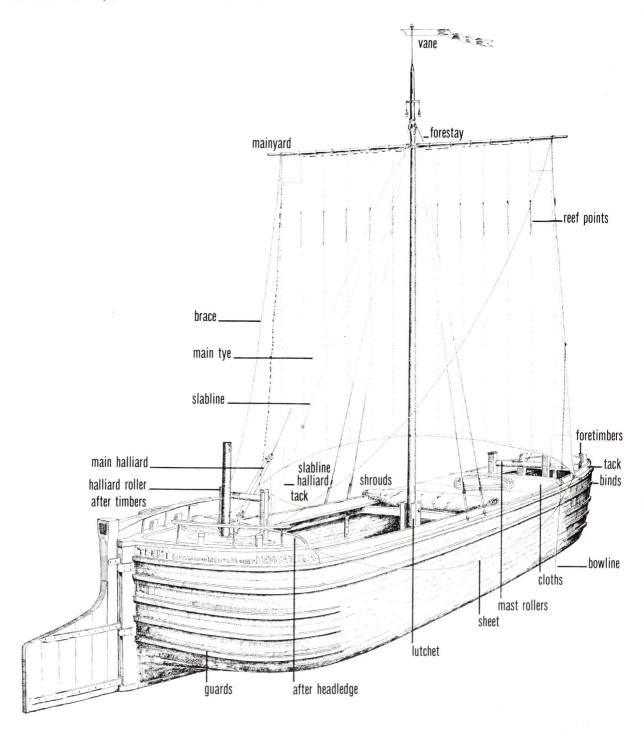

vane

forestay

mainyard

reef points

brace

main tye

slabline

foretimbers

main halliard

slabline

tack

halliard roller
after timbers

halliard
tack

shrouds

binds

bowline

cloths

mast rollers

sheet

lutchet

guards

after headledge

73 A head-on view of an Upper Trent boat, with the mainsail hauled up by the slabline, a method of spilling the wind. They had the mast and halliard rollers of a keel, but were only decked aft.

74 The photograph shows non tidal dumb boats operated by the Leeds Industrial Co-operative Society in their coal traffic from the Aireside pits to their Leeds wharf, which lasted until 1975. The later ones, like these, were steel-built in the 1920s and '30s, mostly by Richard Dunston of Thorne. They measured 61ft 6in by 14ft 9in with a 6ft 6in draft, and could carry 100 tons.

75 A scene in the Goole barge dock in the 1900s, crowded with keels and sailing vessels. Prominent in the foreground are some Aire and Calder Navigation Company fly-boats with their distinctive markings and lettering 'Licensed Fly-Boat'. They were tug towed, some of which are evident in the background.

76

77

76 A magnificent view of the River Ouse at York when commercial traffic was at its height, probably in the 1890s. There are many sailing keels in the foreground and a steam keel in the middle distance, which was possibly one of Henry Leetham's, the York flour millers, having a capacity of 150 tons.

77 Steam keels were introduced in 1852 by the Aire and Calder Navigation as cargo carrying tugs to handle their own carrying fleet. Later examples varied much in size from the four 150-ton capacity ones owned by Henry Leetham and Sons Ltd, the York flour millers, which brought grain from Hull docks, to a quite small steam-cum-sail keel on the Driffield Navigation. Five steam keels were owned by Rishworth, Ingleby and Lofthouse Ltd, the Hull flour millers; this is a model of their *Eagle* built at Hessle in 1905, 85ft long by 17ft beam. These craft were given compound engines and return tube 'Scotch' boilers situated aft, the captain, mate and engineer berthing forward. Note the compass binnacle in the wheel box. Some steam keels ran fly services up the Barnsley Canal into the early 1950s.

78 An unidentified steam keel on the River Hull, a scene which was probably taken in the 1900s, and copied from a $3\frac{1}{4} \times 3\frac{1}{4}$in lantern slide.

79 Sheffield basin in the 1950s with an assembly of Sheffield size craft (61ft 6in by 15ft 6in), some powered, some dumb. All those in the picture are steel built on the lines of the old keels, and indeed some could be ex-sailing keels.

Trent Navigation Company's Steel River Craft

Yare *was one of a fleet of steel motor river craft introduced from 1929. She was built by Watson's of Gainsborough, 82ft 6in long with a capacity of 100 tons.*

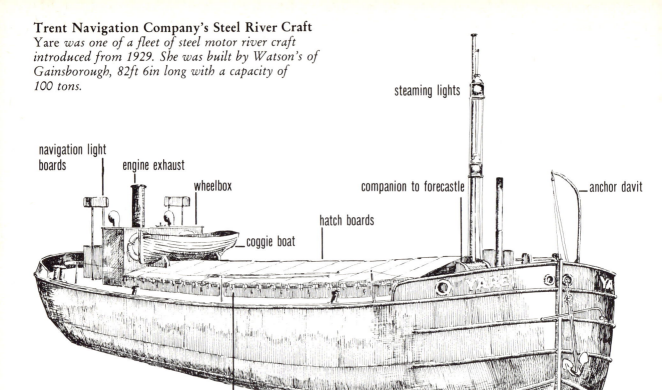

navigation light boards

engine exhaust

wheelbox

coggie boat

hatch boards

steaming lights

companion to forecastle

anchor davit

coamings

80

80 After the river improvements in the 1920s the Trent Navigation Company embarked on a fleet of motor barges, the first being the *Stort* launched by Watson's of Gainsborough in 1929. She was the same length, 82ft 6in, as a Trent pan or dumb barge, and had a 60hp Kromhout engine. Other motor craft of similar size followed, mostly named after rivers. This is one of them below Keadby Bridge. They had a capacity of some 100 tons, and could tow up to two pans.

81 Nowadays motor craft are universal in Yorkshire. Many old sailing keels and sloops were unrigged and fitted with oil engines, some keeping their sails for a while with the engine as an auxiliary. Only one or two of these are left, including the Humber Keel and Sloop Preservation Society's *Comrade* now restored to a keel's square rig. New craft followed keel hull form and dimensions, although stern design has altered to improve flow to the propeller and check cavitation, which occurs when a propeller loses efficiency by working in a mixture of air and water. Traditional in appearance however is Ernest V. Waddington Ltd's *Enterprise*, a 'Sheffield-size' craft here seen at Waddington's Eastwood wharf near Rotherham. She can carry up to 100 tons.

Tanker Craft

Humber Pride *built in 1979 by the Yorkshire Dry Dock Company Ltd, at Hull for John H. Whitaker the Hull river craft operators. Humber Pride and her sister ship Humber Jubilee can carry 600 tons of oil each and normally work from Hull up the Aire and Calder Navigation to Leeds. They measure 199ft 4in long overall, by 19ft 8¼in breadth, with a loaded draught of 8ft. Propulsion is by a 320bhp Kelvin engine.*

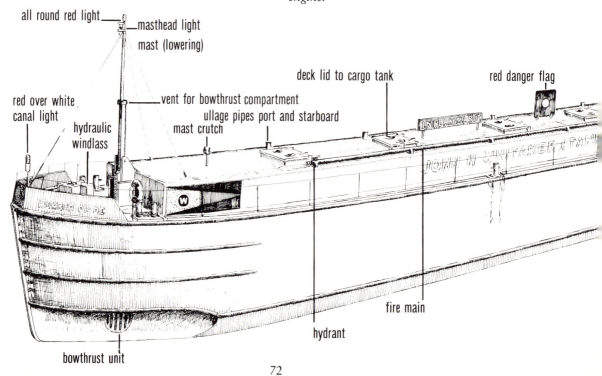

all round red light — masthead light

mast (lowering)

deck lid to cargo tank

red danger flag

red over white canal light

vent for bowthrust compartment

ullage pipes port and starboard

hydraulic windlass

mast crutch

fire main

hydrant

bowthrust unit

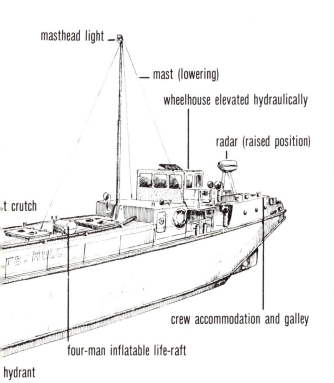

masthead light

mast (lowering)

wheelhouse elevated hydraulically

radar (raised position)

t crutch

crew accommodation and galley

four-man inflatable life-raft

hydrant

82 300 tons of dry cargo is about the maximum capacity of powered river craft on the Ouse, the Aire and Calder Navigation and the Trent below Gainsborough. Recently built craft measure up to 180ft long and are of welded steel with hatch coamings and hatchboards, powered by diesel engines of up to 160hp. Older craft have been lengthened by the insertion of a new midship section. *Risby* of Flixborough Shipping Ltd, Keadby, was built in 1968 by John Harker of Knottingley, and has a 122hp Kelvin engine. The Continental practice of taking one's car aboard is copied by her captain on his way down from Parkhill Colliery, Wakefield, with 300 tons of coal. The photograph was taken on the Stanley Ferry aqueduct.

83 Inevitably oil has become a major Yorkshire cargo and the Leeds line of the Aire and Calder Navigation passes tanker barges of up to 600 tons capacity. John Harker Ltd of Knottingley were pioneers of self-propelled tank barges in the 1920s and many have since been built by them. This is their 250-ton capacity refined-spirit tanker *Lonsdale H* at Ferrybridge, at the entrance to the Knottingley-Goole Canal in May 1957. She was built in 1948 at Harker's Knottingley shipyard.

84 and **85**   John Harker Ltd also built *Bilsdale H*
(above) of 250 tons capacity in 1952, and *Rufus
Stone* (below) of 480 tons in 1963. Both were designed
to carry refined spirit, which being lighter than
crude oil, needs more stowage for the vessel to
achieve her full tonnage, so the cargo pumps are on
deck forward of the wheelhouse.

86 John Harker's shipyard at Knottingley on the Aire and Calder Navigation showing two river craft fitting out for Harker's own fleet and a coastal tanker on the building berth. Harker's took over the yard in 1929 and continue to build ships and inland craft, although most of their tanker carrying fleet has now been sold off.

87 The buffet and bedhole of a Trent barge, *Cressy T.* The buffet (to the right) was the set of cupboards and lockers right up against the stern. Keel cabins were obviously much roomier than a narrow boat's but likewise ingenious, although not so decorative, the ornamentation being confined to graining, and some moulding and carved work.

6 The Leeds and Liverpool Canal and the Lancaster Canal

Crossing the Pennines to link the Mersey with the Aire, the Leeds and Liverpool Canal was built broad to accommodate the types of craft in use at each end, flats in Lancashire, keels in Yorkshire. More consideration was given to the keels, however, because only the locks at the Liverpool end, up to Wigan, were long enough for the flats which were using the old Douglas Navigation, by-passed by the canal. In fact the Leeds and Liverpool Canal produced its own style of craft, of keel shape, but much shallower than the keel and open holded with tarpaulin covers. These were the 62ft by 14ft 3in 'short' boats, but there were also plenty of 72ft 'long' boats, built to the same model, which were restricted to the Liverpool end. All Leeds and Liverpool Canal craft were round bilged with longitudinal bottom planking, following the flat and keel pattern, and very many were square sterned, a flat feature. Fly-boats, however, were always round sterned and the round stern was retained by the steamers and motor boats with no real modifications, for in the steamers at any rate the propeller was sited outboard of the sternpost with the rudder on extension brackets.

88 Leeds and Liverpool Canal boat horse 'Tim' with young Harry Lawson, and in the background the 72ft-boat *Leo*, of H. and R. Ainscough's fleet, the corn millers of Parbold and Burscough. The setting is Scarisbrick Wood in the 1930s. Leeds and Liverpool Canal horses had leather tubes over the traces to protect both the horse and the traces from chafe.

One class of Leeds and Liverpool Canal boat exhibited considerable refinements, namely the fleet built in the 1930s and '40s for H. and R. Ainscough, the Parbold and Burscough millers. These were motor and dumb pairs, 72ft long, with coamings and hatch boards because they had to cross the Mersey to Birkenhead Docks for grain cargoes.

Lancaster Canal boats were very like those on the Leeds and Liverpool Canal, built to fit the longer locks on the Lancaster Canal. All were given square sterns and many were built of iron, because repair facilities were few on this canal.

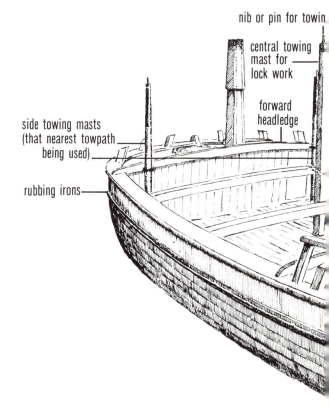

nib or pin for towin

central towing mast for lock work

forward headledge

side towing masts (that nearest towpath being used)

rubbing irons

Leeds and Liverpool Canal Horse-Drawn Short Boat
A typical Leeds and Liverpool wooden 'short' boat built on the Yorkshire side, with a square stern and Humber keel style wooden stove chimneys.

89 Wooden Leeds and Liverpool Canal boats were built in the same way as barges, with closely spaced frames or timbers, and planking laid parallel to the keel, unlike narrow boats which had few frames, cross boarded flat bottoms and square bilges. This view of a short boat under repair at James Mayor's yard at Tarleton on the Douglas Navigation in 1957 shows the planking and framing and the round bilge of these craft. Compared with a narrow boat with relatively few planks, the many narrow planks of a short boat needed constant watching for leaky seams and consequently plenty of work with the caulking mallet. Mayor's built canal craft at Wigan and Tarleton and are still very much in business at the latter yard.

89

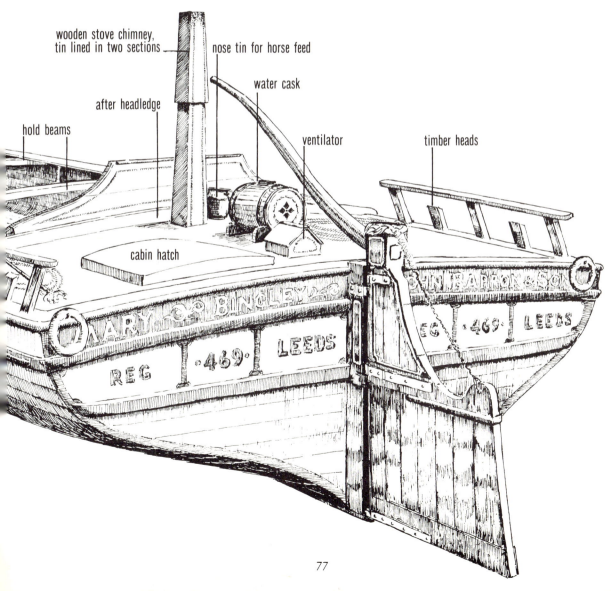

wooden stove chimney, tin lined in two sections

nose tin for horse feed

water cask

after headledge

ventilator

timber heads

hold beams

cabin hatch

REG ·469· LEEDS

90 On the Yorkshire side Leeds and Liverpool Canal craft had several marked keel features, such as the method of framing and more obviously the square-section wooden (but tin lined) chimneys built up in sections and the nicely curved board above the headledge to contain the cargo. The boat seen here is leaving Hurst Lock, Shipley going towards Bingley. Note the water barrel, the cabin ventilator and the three towing masts, the centre one for lock work, and the side ones for normal haulage, that nearest the towpath being selected. Masts were carried in short and long sizes depending on whether the boat was full or empty, the long making it easier to clear the line over an approaching boat. A full boat could carry 40 tons of coal on a draught of 3ft 6in.

91 Long boats were simply longer than short boats, and like the latter some had round, some square sterns. It was always 'square stern' in the north, not 'transom'. Many were open coal boats, loading up to 70 tons on a 5ft draught, working between the Wigan and Leigh pits to Liverpool and Manchester and onto the Bridgewater Canal, the boats being called Wiganers. T. and W. Wells Ltd of Wigan and later of Stretford had a large fleet, some acquired from the Wigan Coal and Iron Company of which *Leeds* was one, seen crossing the Barton swing aqueduct in August 1956.

92 Steam tugs were introduced to the Leeds and Liverpool Canal in 1871 to tow coal boats on the long pound of 29¼ miles between Appley Bridge and Liverpool. Then came plans to convert the long coal boats themselves to steam and in 1880 four steam fly-boats were ordered for the Leeds and Liverpool Canal's own carrying fleet. They were mostly short boats, narrower by a foot than the horse boats, so they were faster. Eventually there were forty-six of them, short and long, originally named, later numbered. The short ones only carried 30 tons, sacrificing 10 tons for the vee tandem-compound engine and boiler, hence the need to work fly, towing two or three horse boats. Here is a scene taken in 1935, by which time the Leeds and Liverpool Canal themselves had given up carrying (in 1921), although since 1930 they had invested in Canal Transport Ltd, formed by the amalgamated fleets of three private carriers who had bought up much of the old Leeds and Liverpool Canal carrying fleet, including this steamer.

90

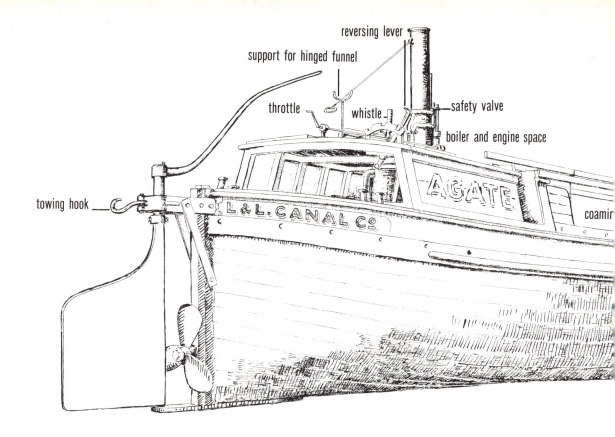

support for hinged funnel
reversing lever
throttle
whistle
safety valve
boiler and engine space
towing hook
L&L. CANAL Cº
AGATE
coamir

93

Leeds and Liverpool Canal Steam Fly-Boat

A wooden-hulled steam fly-boat designed to tow dumb craft over the summit. Length 62ft, breadth 13ft.

94

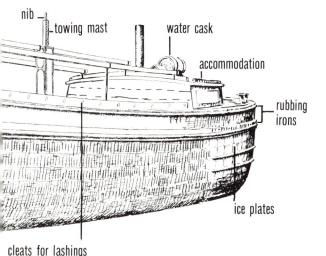

nib

towing mast

water cask

accommodation

rubbing irons

ice plates

cleats for lashings

93 One of John Robert Thornton of Skipton's two steamers, possibly the *Florence*. The funnel is hinged for low bridges, and on the right is the reversing lever, while the steerer is holding the throttle.

94 The engine of a Leeds and Liverpool Canal steam fly-boat, a vee tandem-compound with high- and low-pressure cylinders sharing a common piston rod and valve spindle. The vertical boiler is immediately in front of the engine.

95 Before World War I the Leeds and Liverpool Canal Company was experimenting with an oil engine in an ex-steamer, but no further work was done until the 1920s. Several private carriers then had horse boats converted and new motor boats built, using the Widdop engine made at Keighley. Between 1930 and 1952 Canal Transport Ltd ordered a series of steel and wooden motor short boats, one of which was *Ribble*, completed by W.J. Yarwood of Northwich in 1934. The picture, taken at the shipyard, shows the stands and sheeting rails for tarpaulin covers.

95

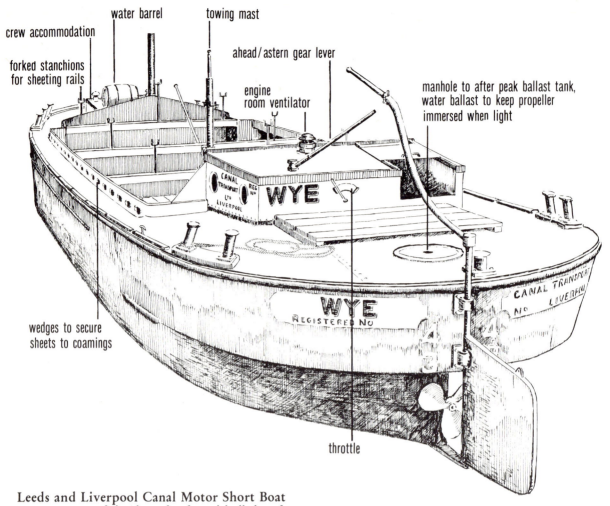

crew accommodation

water barrel

towing mast

forked stanchions
for sheeting rails

ahead/astern gear lever

engine
room ventilator

manhole to after peak ballast tank,
water ballast to keep propeller
immersed when light

CANAL
TRANSPORT
LTD
LIVERPOOL

REG
No.

WYE

WYE
REGISTERED No

CANAL TRANSPORT
No   LIVERPOOL

wedges to secure
sheets to coamings

throttle

Leeds and Liverpool Canal Motor Short Boat
Wye *was one of the class of 61ft steel-hulled craft
built during the 1930s and '40s for Canal Transport
Ltd, of Liverpool.* Wye *was completed by W.J. Yarwood at Northwich in 1947.*

96 Built by Harland and Wolff, North Woolwich,
in 1952, *Everton* was the second of three British
Waterways Leeds and Liverpool Canal short boats
to be built of high-tensile steel with a beam of 14ft
6in and a 4ft laden draught. As a consequence of
these modifications 10 per cent more cargo could
be carried. The other two of the series were named
Darwen and *Farnworth* and they remained in nation-
alized commercial service until 1963 when British
Waterways gave up their Leeds and Liverpool
Canal carrying activities. This is the stretch of
canal between Liverpool and Bootle spanned by the
power transmission lines from Clarence Dock power
station.

97 Larger 72ft steel motor and dumb craft were
built at Yarwood's for H. and R. Ainscough, the
Parbold and Burscough millers, to bring grain from
Liverpool and Birkenhead docks. So they had to
cross the Mersey and were given detachable side
rails, high hatch coamings and hatch boards, also an
anchor, life buoys and navigation lights, the last on
long stalks so that they were easily seen. *Attractive*
was a dumb barge, and *Ironclad* a motor, with a
24bhp Widdop engine. Cargo capacity was 60 tons
of grain, both boats being delivered in 1933. The
names were taken from the company's fine Shire
horses.

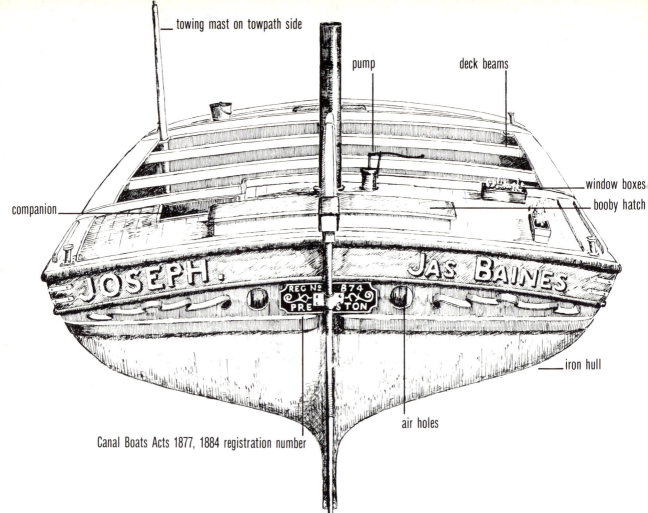

towing mast on towpath side

pump

deck beams

companion

window boxes

booby hatch

JOSEPH.   JAS BAINES

REG Nº B74 PRESTON

iron hull

air holes

Canal Boats Acts 1877, 1884 registration number

Lancaster Canal Boat

Boats on the Lancaster Canal were mostly built of iron by W. Allsupp and Sons at Preston. Delivery to the canal had to be round the coast to Glasson Dock, as there was no canal-river link in Preston. Baines was the largest carrier in the latter days of traffic.

98   Repair facilities were few on the Lancaster Canal and during the nineteenth century wooden craft gave way to iron and steel which needed less attention. They were built on the Ribble at Preston by W. Allsup and Sons and towed round to

Glasson Dock. Lancaster Canal boats measured up to 77ft long by 14ft 6in wide and could carry 50 tons of coal. All had square sterns and all were horse drawn, some with two horses, apart from a couple of Leeds and Liverpool Canal steamers. Ashcrofts' were the last carriers and this is one of their boats at Hest Bank, north of Lancaster.

99   Decoration on Leeds and Liverpool Canal craft was a mixture of geometric and scroll work and reached its zenith on the square sterns. *Joan* was repainted in June 1951 by T. and W. Wells at their Stretford yard, which they had bought from Rathbone's in 1932. The painter was the yard manager Harry Leyland, *Joan* herself being a short boat built on the Yorkshire side.

100   The richly decorated stern of the 72ft Leeds and Liverpool Canal boat *Richard*, owned by Richard Williams and Sons Ltd of Liverpool. The colour scheme of this fleet was red, white and blue with a little green. *Richard* was exceptionally well decorated, probably because she bore the christian name of the owner, and this picture which dates from the 1940s shows the boat on the canal at Litherland. Note the spare tiller.

7 North-Western Craft

North-West England bred its own type of river and canal boat based on those traditional river barges of the Mersey, the flats. These were an old type whose origins are uncertain, probably square rigged and double ended. Later, certainly in the eighteenth century, the square stern appeared, a hallmark of flat design for a hundred years. When the rivers were improved and the canals built, the locks and bridges were constructed to flat dimensions. Now the craft of the Mersey were able to extend their operations, up to Manchester, Winsford, St Helens and eventually Rochdale and the West Riding of Yorkshire. Flats built on the canals, starting with the Bridgewater, evolved their own characteristics, a particular feature being the need to design a hull which would combine shallow draught with a worthwhile cargo space. This was a very necessary consideration on the Rochdale Canal, while craft which worked through onto the Calder and Hebble Navigation had to be short enough to fit the locks on that waterway.

Power craft on the Mersey and associated waterways followed a fairly standard design. Steamers, introduced in the mid nineteenth century, used a hull based on the shape of a sailing flat with the rudder hung outboard, but motor craft employed the counter stern, and looked more or less like their sisters in Yorkshire and on the Severn.

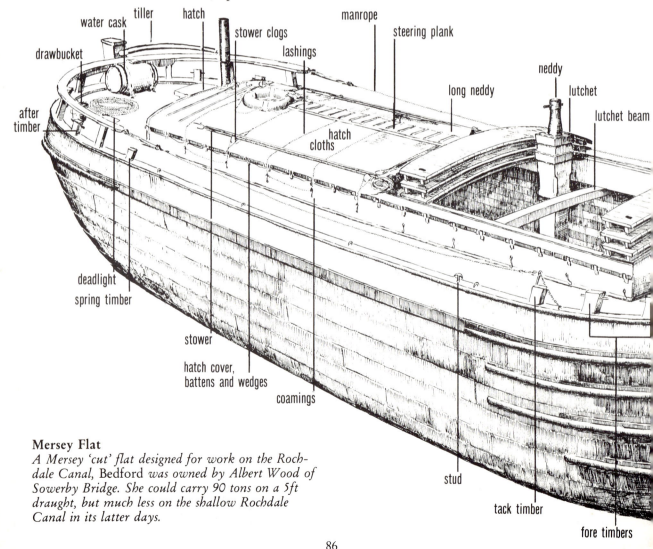

water cask · tiller · hatch · stower clogs · manrope · steering plank · lashings · drawbucket · neddy · long neddy · lutchet · lutchet beam · after timber · hatch cloths · deadlight · spring timber · stower · hatch cover, battens and wedges · coamings · stud · tack timber · fore timbers

Mersey Flat

A Mersey 'cut' flat designed for work on the Rochdale Canal, Bedford was owned by Albert Wood of Sowerby Bridge. She could carry 90 tons on a 5ft draught, but much less on the shallow Rochdale Canal in its latter days.

101

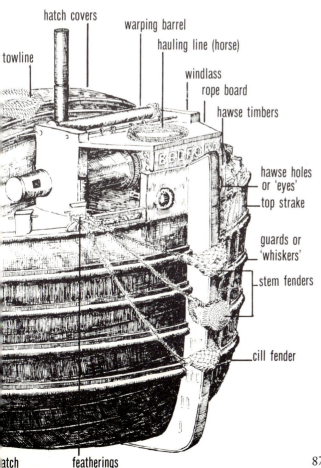

towline
hatch covers
warping barrel
hauling line (horse)
windlass
rope board
hawse timbers
hawse holes or 'eyes'
top strake
guards or 'whiskers'
stem fenders
cill fender
hatch
featherings

101 Yorkshire waterways had three direct links with those of Lancashire; via the narrow Huddersfield Canal; via the long Leeds and Liverpool Canal, and via the short but heavily locked Rochdale Canal, with 92 locks from Manchester to Sowerby Bridge, which was the junction with the Calder and Hebble Navigation. The Rochdale Canal was designed not only for Yorkshire keels of Calder and Hebble size, but for the 72ft-long Mersey flats which used the Bridgewater (the canal the Rochdale joined in Manchester), and the Mersey itself. After an early venture into carrying, the Rochdale Canal Company revived a fleet in 1888 with steam and horse drawn craft; by 1892 they had fifteen steam packets, fifteen flats and keels, the latter similar to the *Emily* (plate 65) and thirty-eight narrow boats. They stayed in business until 1921 when high costs, high wages and the eight hour day forced them out. One of the last cargoes was cotton to Lockhill Mills, Sowerby Bridge, unloaded from the flat *Primrose* on 3 June 1921. The Rochdale variety of Mersey canal or 'cut' flat measured 72ft long by 13ft 6in beam and could carry 80-90 tons on a laden draught of 5ft, but the shallow Rochdale Canal allowed less than 4ft and only 40 tons in its latter days.

102

103

104

102 Rochdale Canal Company iron-hulled steam packets were named after rivers and *Tyne* is seen here on the Manchester Ship Canal opposite No 9 Dock. She had a compound engine and wheel steering, the funnel being hinged for the canal bridges. Of the same hull size she would carry about 10 tons less than a horse hauled flat, nor would she perform so well in a shallow canal. Apart from the smart Ship Canal Company launch, the photograph shows a dredger discharging into one of the container-type spoil boats which Manchester Ship Canal engineers designed for rapid unloading by steam crane, picking up each box in turn and tipping it.

103 Flats were the principal carriers on the Bridgewater Canal, the Duke himself having a near monopoly of traffic. His flats were designed to go under sail on the Mersey from Runcorn to Liverpool and this dual river/canal role was continued by his successors, Bridgewater Canal craft being called 'dukers'. Duker flats were wall-sided with less shape than, for example, a Shropshire Union Canal flat. They came in three sizes, or depths, for all had about the same length and breadth, not less than 71ft by 14ft 3in; Birkenhead flats were purely Mersey craft, never entering the Bridgewater Canal; Preston flats went up as far as Preston Brook; but Manchester flats the whole way. 80 tons on a 4ft draught was the maximum canal capacity, with 90 tons and 5ft laden draught on the Mersey. Here a duker is unloading at the top of Runcorn Locks.

104 Many larger canal carrying companies had their own repair yards and some even built their own vessels. The Bridgewater Department of the Manchester Ship Canal Company inherited the Sprinch yard at Runcorn from their predecessors the Bridgewater Navigation Company. Here in 1911 they built the 'duker' *Coronation* (it was the Coronation Year of George V and Queen Mary), but no more than three new craft were built at the Sprinch yard, although there were eight dry docks for repairs.

105

106

105 A broadside view of the duker *Coronation* before her launch in 1911 at the Sprinch, Runcorn. The hull is held by a pair of blocks, both cleared simultaneously.

106 Mersey canal or 'cut' flats worked up the Shropshire Union Canal from Ellesmere Port to Chester and Nantwich, the Shropshire Union Canal Company themselves having a large fleet of 103 in 1898, with steam tugs both on the Mersey and between Ellesmere Port and Chester. Their flats were more rounded than the dukers or Bridgewater Canal ones, so would swim better in a shallow canal. This one, *Mossdale* was probably built in the 1870s at Chester. Her name then was *Ruby*, but the Shropshire Union Canal sold her in 1921 when they gave up carrying and her new owners renamed her. Now she is preserved by the North West Museum of Inland Navigation at Ellesmere Port, after extensive repair in the Weaver Navigation dock at Northwich, the scene of this picture.

107 Wooden flats continued to be built in the 1920s, for example by J.H. Taylor and Sons of Chester who launched some for the Wolverhampton Corrugated Iron Company, who had a steelworks at Ellesmere Port. Note the cabin ventilator and the nicely shaped tiller; behind is the Shropshire Union Canal Company's dry dock, leased by Taylor's.

107

108

108 J.H. Taylor and Sons also built wooden floats for the Wolverhampton Corrugated Iron Company. These were fully decked craft for deck cargoes only of steel sections and fabrications and sheets of galvanized iron. Each was given the prefix *Elles*, like all the Corrugated Iron Company boats. This is *Ellesmanor*. The Shropshire Union Canal had similar floats named after trees, and there were others on the Bridgewater Canal.

109 There were probably sailing barges on the Mersey in medieval times, doubtless with a single square sail, but during the eighteenth century this was being replaced by the more handy fore-and-aft rig. They worked within river limits and did short coastal passages up the Lancashire coast and down the Welsh coast with trips over to the Isle of Man and Ireland. When river navigations were improved and canals built the sailing flat went inland; up to Manchester via the Mersey and Irwell Navigation; up the River Weaver; up the Sankey Brook Navigation to the pits near St Helens, and up the Douglas Navigation to the Wigan coalfield. They could rarely sail on these inland waterways and they had to lower their masts for bridges. On pure canals like the Bridgewater they were horse hauled or later towed by steam and motor tugs. Many were then unrigged and many more built as canal or 'cut' flats, a vast family of craft which worked from

Liverpool and Birkenhead Docks along canals like the Rochdale, the Leeds and Liverpool and the Shropshire Union. The sailing flat survived as a river and coastal trader as late as the 1930s, one lasting until 1954. Some were large ketch-rigged craft with capacities of 175 tons, but these are smaller, say of 100 tons capacity, in West Bank Dock, Widnes, before 1914.

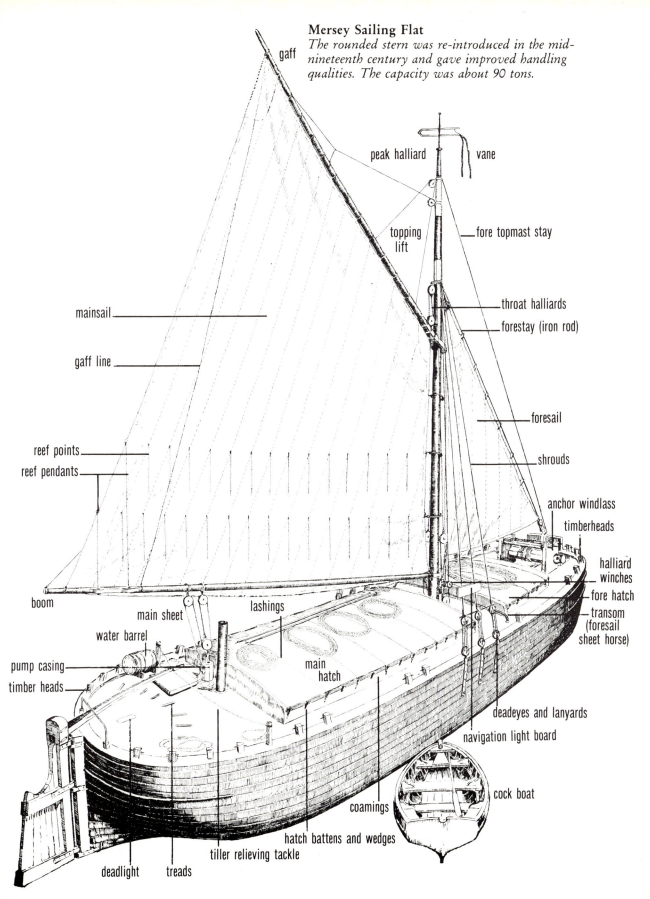

Mersey Sailing Flat
*The rounded stern was re-introduced in the mid-
nineteenth century and gave improved handling
qualities. The capacity was about 90 tons.*

gaff

peak halliard

vane

topping
lift

fore topmast stay

mainsail

throat halliards

forestay (iron rod)

gaff line

foresail

shrouds

reef points

reef pendants

anchor windlass

timberheads

halliard
winches

fore hatch

boom

transom
(foresail
sheet horse)

main sheet

lashings

water barrel

pump casing

main
hatch

timber heads

deadeyes and lanyards

navigation light board

cock boat

coamings

hatch battens and wedges

tiller relieving tackle

deadlight

treads

110

110 A rare close-up view of a Mersey flat under sail, one of the earlier square sterned ones. She is just off the entrance to Canning Dock, Liverpool, and the date is about 1908. Note the rail (flats never had bulwarks) and the large diameter blocks for free running gear, much of it chain.

111 The Weston Canal, completed in 1810, made a new outlet for the Weaver Navigation at Weston Point. This view shows the last few yards of the canal as it reaches Weston Point Docks, with Christ Church, built in 1841 by the Weaver Trustees as a boatman's church, in the background. Behind the maintenance boat in the foreground is a smart Mersey flat, freshly tarred.

111

112

112 A watercolour of a ketch or jigger-rigged Mersey flat under all plain sail, including the rarely set topsail. This was *Petrel* built in 1873 at Northwich and at one time owned by the Liverpool Lighterage Company.

113 Square sterns were universal on Mersey and Weaver sailing flats until the mid-nineteenth century; thereafter Mersey craft reverted to the much earlier rounded stern, but those on the Weaver kept their square one. This was because no new sailing flats were built for the Weaver Navigation, for the steam packets were rapidly putting them out of business. The square stern shape was easier and cheaper to build and did make full use of the dimensions allowed by locks, but was probably less handy to steer. One survival was the flat *Daresbury* built in the eighteenth century but for a long time a lifting craft used by the Weaver Navigation. She was eventually sunk or beached in 1958, but not before full details of her construction had been recorded.

114 Whereas stern shape was important for steerage and in a sailing barge for efficient handling, particularly for going about when tacking, a barge's bow could be built bluff to make full use of hold space. Yorkshire keels have bows which are almost square with rounded corners, and Mersey flats were similar. This is the bow of *Daresbury* photographed below Hunt's Locks, Northwich in 1957.

113

114

115　Salt traffic on the Weaver Navigation went over to steam in the 1860s, with steam tugs introduced in 1863 and in December of that year the cargo carrying steamer *Experiment* was launched by Falk's the Winsford salt producers. She was designed to tow up to three flats and this became standard practice in the salt trade. More steamers or packets were commissioned when the Brunner Mond chemical works at Winnington were founded and expanded, their first being delivered in 1889. Some Brunner Mond craft were wooden hulled, the later ones steel, *Gwalia* (illustrated below Hunt's Locks, Northwich) of 1908 being the last built with a wooden hull. As successors to Brunner Mond, and in 1937 acquiring the Salt Union fleet, Imperial Chemical Industries operated Weaver steam packets until 1967, and still run motor barges, also called packets. The steamers varied much in size, the smaller Salt Union ones carrying 170 tons, the largest Brunner Mond 285 tons.

116　Built by Falk's of Winsford for their own fleet of salt packets, *Opus* is believed to have been fabricated from old iron salt pans with stem and stern posts made up of railway line. Falk's were the pioneers of steam on the Weaver in the 1860s. *Opus* remained with the Salt Union and ICI until 1961 when she passed to Richard Abel of Liverpool for conversion into a sand barge. Her capacity was about 200 tons of salt. She is entering Hunt's Locks, Northwich on her way to Winsford; behind her are two more packets, *Scotia* and *Caledonia* with Yarwood's shipyard in the background.

116

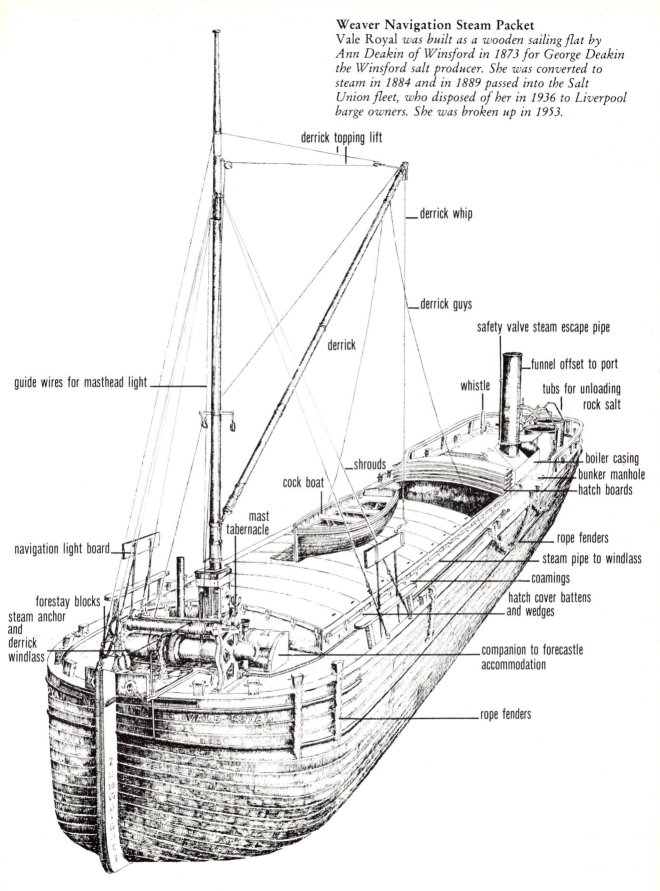

Weaver Navigation Steam Packet
Vale Royal *was built as a wooden sailing flat by Ann Deakin of Winsford in 1873 for George Deakin the Winsford salt producer. She was converted to steam in 1884 and in 1889 passed into the Salt Union fleet, who disposed of her in 1936 to Liverpool barge owners. She was broken up in 1953.*

derrick topping lift

derrick whip

derrick guys

derrick

safety valve steam escape pipe

funnel offset to port

tubs for unloading rock salt

whistle

guide wires for masthead light

boiler casing

bunker manhole

hatch boards

shrouds

cock boat

rope fenders

steam pipe to windlass

coamings

mast tabernacle

navigation light board

hatch cover battens and wedges

forestay blocks

steam anchor and derrick windlass

companion to forecastle accommodation

rope fenders

VALE ROYAL

99

117

118

CESTRIA

119

117 One of the most powerful of the Weaver steam packets, *Herald of Peace* was built of iron in 1877 by John Thompson at Northwich for his own salt carrying fleet. Later she passed to the Salt Union and finally to ICI. She was much in demand as a tug and in this picture is towing a flat upstream from Hunt's Locks, Northwich. The engine was two cylinder simple-expansion, the cylinders arranged in a vee.

118 Griffiths' corn mills on the canal at Chester had three steam barges between the wars, *Anglia, Cambria* and *Cestria*. They may possibly have come from the Rochdale Canal Company's fleet when they gave up carrying in 1921. This view of *Cestria* at J.H. Taylor and Sons yard at Chester, the former Shropshire Union dock, shows how an iron vessel is assembled, angled frames and plates, bulkheads, all punched with many, many holes for the rivets. Welding has cut out this elaborate work.

119 The Bridgewater Canal had no powered cargo craft until 1951-2, when four barges were built by Isaac Pimblott and two by W.J. Yarwood of Northwich. The first was *Paradine*, all being given the prefix *Par*. She had a 68hp Gardner engine and could carry 80 tons. Steel dumb barges of 114 tons capacity were built at about the same time by the same two builders, and here, in April 1961, *Parderry* and one of the dumb barges, all named after Cheshire and Shropshire meres, lie on the Runcorn and Latchford Canal above Twenty Steps Lock, where the old waterway (this section generally called the Black Bear Canal) meets the Manchester Ship Canal.

120 With the increasing use of iron and later steel for river and canal craft building, larger shipyards took a hand in the work. They had the capital for the equipment needed for metal fabrication: plating furnaces, shearing machines, frame bending blocks and so on. One firm which gained large canal craft contracts was W.J. Yarwood and Sons of Northwich, which between the wars built no less than 213 narrow boats for Fellows, Morton and Clayton, the Grand Union Canal Carrying Company, and other owners. This picture, taken in 1921, shows barges fitting out for the Wolverhampton Corrugated Iron Company, who had a steelworks at Ellesmere Port, hence their names, all starting with *Elles*. *Ellesborough* was a steam barge, the remainder dumb. Under repair on the slip is the steam packet *Thistle* built for Brunner Mond and Company Ltd, in 1890.

121 The Wolverhampton Corrugated Iron Company changed from steam to motor power in the mid 1920s. *Ellesport* was their first, completed by Yarwood's of Northwich in 1925 with a four cylinder Gardner semi-diesel engine of 72bhp. She was fitted out for towing dumb barges of the fleet, mainly on the Mersey, and is here seen at Taylor's dock in Chester.

120

122 At Sankey Bridges on the St Helens Canal in 1956, is one of the sugar barges running to the Sankey sugar refinery at Earlestown, a traffic which lasted until 1959. At that time owned by Rea's of Liverpool, *Ellesweir* started life in 1924, built as a steamer by W.J. Yarwood of Northwich for the Wolverhampton Corrugated Iron Company's steel-works at Ellesmere Port. She could carry up to 100 tons.

8 Scottish Craft

The principal Scottish canals, the Forth and Clyde, the Caledonian, and the Crinan, were designed for sea-going ships, but the Forth and Clyde was fed by tributary waterways which were purely inland navigations. Scow was the generic term for Scots canal craft: mineral scows, timber scows and so on, some open holded, some with hatch covers. These scows were the ancestors of the famous Clyde puffers, for some were fitted with steam engines and a derrick, and later bulwarks, so that they could go into the Clyde and

Forth and eventually become coasters, serving the Highlands and Islands. As coasters they replaced the sailing gabbarts, although some of the larger gabbarts survived in traffic alongside the puffers.

The only Scottish 'narrow boats' were those on the Glasgow, Paisley and Johnstone Canal. They were not like English narrow boats but were scows built to the comparatively small dimensions of this canal, that is, small compared with the Forth and Clyde Canal and the Monkland Canal.

123 Drawn by two heavy horses, a pit prop laden scow works up the locks of the Forth and Clyde Canal near Camelon on the outskirts of Falkirk. Scow was the name for cargo carrying craft on the Forth and Clyde, and the Union and Monkland Canals; many were open holded carrying minerals, others were given hatch boards. They measured some 60ft long by 13ft 6in beam (a foot narrower for the Union Canal) and could carry 70 to 80 tons on a 5 to 6ft draught. Many were iron, the first iron ones being built in the 1820s. Latterly steel scows were built, the last in 1948, by which time horse traction was nearly ended.

124 Sailing barges on the Firth of Clyde were called gabbarts, confusing because a gabbart could also be a dumb lighter, working between Greenock and Glasgow. In the eighteenth century the latter were of small capacity but were enlarged when the river was improved. Sailing gabbarts were fore and

aft rigged with gaff mainsail and foresail and measured about 60ft long by 13ft 6in beam, with a laden draught of up to 6ft. They used the Forth and Clyde Canal and the Monkland Canal, lowering their masts for the latter's fixed bridges and worked up as far as Oban via the Crinan Canal. Steam puffers supplanted them by the 1900s but larger sailing coasters, smack or ketch rigged, also called gabbarts, lasted longer. This is a much used scene of the *Mary* (built 1845) in the Holy Loch, but this is one of the few gabbart pictures to have survived. Note the heavy wooden fenders.

125 A postcard view of Lock 16 on the Forth and Clyde Canal, at the junction with the Edinburgh and Glasgow Union Canal. The vessel is a bit of a problem. She must be a sailing gabbart in charge of a horse which is invisible in the picture, and indeed she has been identified as the *Flash*. The chimney is too small for a puffer.

123

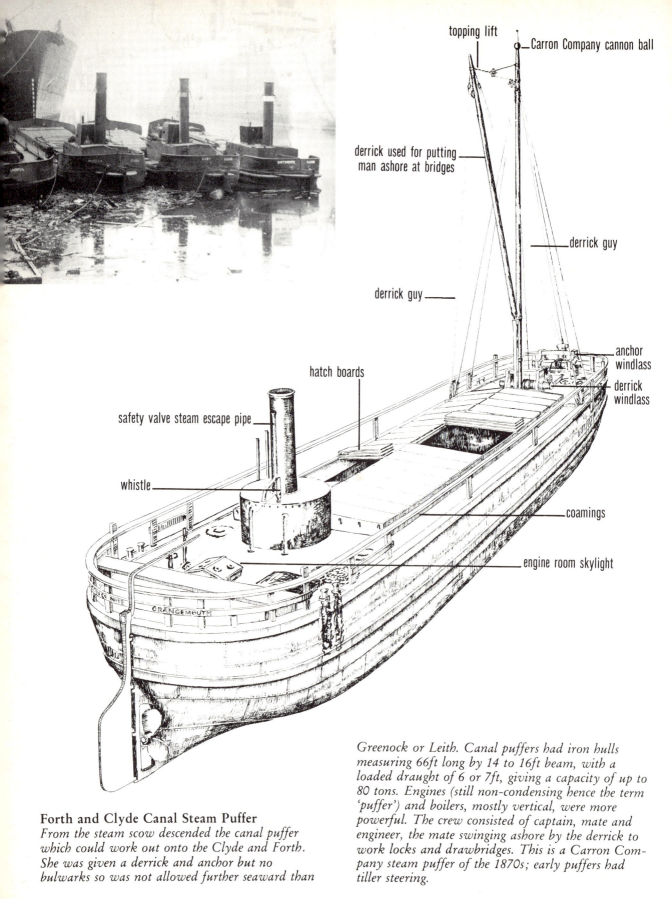

topping lift

Carron Company cannon ball

derrick used for putting
man ashore at bridges

derrick guy

derrick guy

anchor
windlass

derrick
windlass

hatch boards

safety valve steam escape pipe

coamings

whistle

engine room skylight

GRANGEMOUTH

Forth and Clyde Canal Steam Puffer

*From the steam scow descended the canal puffer
which could work out onto the Clyde and Forth.
She was given a derrick and anchor but no
bulwarks so was not allowed further seaward than*
*Greenock or Leith. Canal puffers had iron hulls
measuring 66ft long by 14 to 16ft beam, with a
loaded draught of 6 or 7ft, giving a capacity of up to
80 tons. Engines (still non-condensing hence the term
'puffer') and boilers, mostly vertical, were more
powerful. The crew consisted of captain, mate and
engineer, the mate swinging ashore by the derrick to
work locks and drawbridges. This is a Carron Company steam puffer of the 1870s; early puffers had
tiller steering.*

126 Steam scows were introduced on the Forth and Clyde Canal in 1856 when the iron *Thomas* was given a two-cylinder simple expansion non-condensing engine. Many more quickly followed on the Forth and Clyde Canal and on the Monkland Canal, but not on the Union Canal because of the low fixed bridges. They were pure canal craft of up to 80 tons capacity although after the 1920s, when the last left the Forth and Clyde Canal, some worked in Glasgow docks as steam suppliers to grain elevators. Three of these scows, *Mary*, *Rebecca* and *Gartsherrie*, all from the Forth and Clyde Canal Company's own carrying fleet, were in use into the 1950s, and are here seen in Prince's dock, Glasgow. The fourth vessel, on the extreme left, was a steam barge from Liverpool.

127 An ex-canal puffer the *Albert* at Bowling, near Dumbarton, alongside a topsail schooner. Note the heavy protective guards on the puffer's hull. She has been given bulwarks so that she could go further afield than Greenock, the normal seaward line for canal puffers. *Albert* was built at Kirkintilloch in 1886 by Hay's for their own fleet.

128 Puffers grew from canal and river craft to become coasting vessels. By 1870 they were being built with bulwarks and sails to save coal, while many canal puffers were 'rose on' or given bulwarks for West Highland services via the Crinan Canal. The *Anzac* approaches the *Pibroch* on the Crinan Canal near Lochgilphead in 1952. Scott's of Bowling built *Anzac* in 1939 for John Hay of Glasgow who had the largest fleet of canal and coastal puffers. *Pibroch* was also built by Scott's, in 1923, for the proprietors of White Horse whisky, to run between Glasgow and their distilleries in Islay.

128

129

129 Whereas the Crinan Canal could take vessels of 85ft in length drawing up to 9ft 6in, the Forth and Clyde Canal limited the length to 66ft. Even so, many coastal puffers continued to use it, and John Hay had a building and repair yard at Kirkintilloch, which was in operation from the late 1860s to 1961. The last puffer to be built there was *Chindit* in 1945 and this 1960 view shows her on the slip with *Anzac* being converted to diesel and *Inca* laid up.

131 Commercial traffic remains on the Lower Bann, from Lough Neagh to a wharf at Toomebridge where the Bann leaves the lough. Sand and gravel are brought by ex-Guinness Liffey barges. This is the *Castlenock*, now dieselized (see plate 136).

9   Irish Craft

Lighter was the general term for the canal craft of Northern Ireland, simply meaning in this instance a decked craft with coamings and hatch covers which could safely navigate the canals, the rivers, the wide expanse of Lough Neagh, and the estuarine waters of the lower Lagan and the Foyle. Other Irish craft were equally versatile although Grand Canal boats did not possess hatch boards and coamings, in spite of the stormy conditions encountered on the Shannon lakes, which they negotiated behind a tug. Some Shannon craft worked under sail carrying turf (peat), but many of the turf boats were simply poled along from the cuttings to the farm or village.

130   Horses were the chief motive power throughout Northern Ireland's waterway history. This is a scene on the Lagan Navigation in the 1940s. All Northern Ireland barges were called lighters, and were wide craft, fully decked with hatches, the cabins being under deck fore and aft, and because those using the Lagan went onto tidal water to the Belfast quays, they carried an anchor and windlass. Dimensions were more or less the same for lighters on the Lagan, the Coalisland Canal and the Newry Navigation, up to 62ft long by 14ft 6in beam carrying up to 80 tons, but the locks of the Ulster Canal would only admit craft of 11ft 6in beam, so special lighters had to be built for it.

Steam and motor propulsion made little impact on Ulster, but steam towage was readily taken up on the River Shannon and on the Grand Canal. The Grand Canal was early in the motor barge field, introducing Bolinder-engined canal craft in 1911, and keeping faith with the Bolinder until the end of traffic in 1960. Their steel motor boats, introduced in the 1920s and 1930s, looked very like Leeds and Liverpool Canal motor boats. Large motor barges, modelled on English craft, were introduced on the Shannon by various operators, but the Guinness steam barges on the River Liffey were distinctive with their hinged funnels and deck cranes.

130

131

132 The oldest of the summit level canals in the
British Isles was the Newry Navigation completed
in 1742. Here one of the Newry lighters, named
Tyrone awaits a cargo, tied up with a sister vessel
alongside the Lagan quays, Belfast. The registration
of the sister lighter with a square stern, cannot be
deciphered. Most impressive is the rank of steamers
berthed at Donegall Quay, serving Ardrossan,
Glasgow, Fleetwood, Heysham and Liverpool. The
date is about 1913.

133   Much of Southern Ireland's Barrow Navigation traffic in grain to the maltings was handled by hack boats, which would be called in England bye traders. The Barrow down to Waterford was a difficult river, liable to floods and the boatmen, the 'Barrow boys', were exceptionally skilled. This is a clinker-built barge owned by James Ryan of Carlow. She would carry about 50 tons, and would be horse drawn but assisted upstream by numerous winches on the bank. The under deck cabin aft is lit by two sliding scuttles, one each side of the stern post. The Barrow Navigation, more or less opened by 1790, and linked by canal to the Grand Canal in 1791, was never as fully improved as had been intended but remains a tourist waterway.

133

Grand Canal Company Motor Boat

One of the large class of steel 15bhp Bolinder-engined boats built in Ireland for the Grand Canal Company. 38M was built in 1928 by the Ringsend Dockyard Company, in Dublin, length 61ft, breadth 13ft.

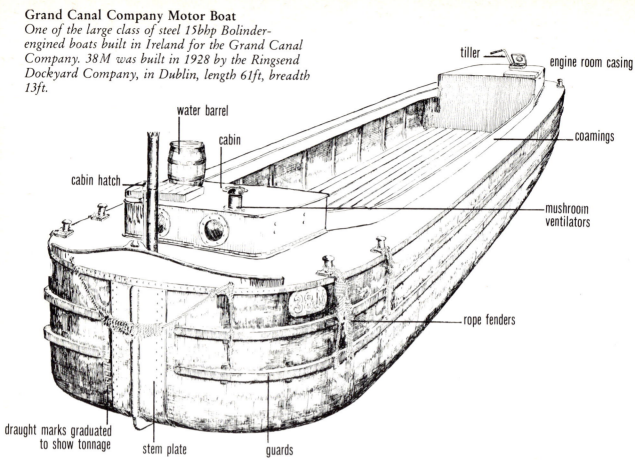

tiller

engine room casing

water barrel

cabin

coamings

cabin hatch

mushroom ventilators

rope fenders

draught marks graduated to show tonnage

stem plate

guards

134

134 Credit for early introduction of the Bolinder semi-diesel engine to the canals of the British Isles must go to the Irish Grand Canal Company who in 1911 converted a horse boat into a motor boat. Many more conversions followed, the craft being renumbered with an M suffix. In 1925 a new series of steel M boats with 15hp Bolinder engines began to be built in Ireland, forty-nine of them, the last in 1939. Very like Leeds and Liverpool Canal motor boats they loaded to 45 tons and were powerful enough to use the Shannon. 35 M was built in 1928, the photograph being taken in 1958 near Roberts-town in Coras Iompair Eireann days. CIE have operated the Grand Canal since 1950.

136 Arthur Guinness Son and Company Ltd provided traffic for the Irish Grand Canal from the early nineteenth century until the last cargoes passed in 1960. On the River Liffey they had their own steam barges working between the St James's Gate Brewery quay (shown here) and the docks. They were named after Dublin suburbs such as *Killiney* and measured 79ft long by 17ft 6in beam with a capacity of 90 tons, and were built at Ross and Walpole's yard on the Liffey. In 1961 the last of the fleet were sold off. Funnels, red with a black top, were offset to starboard and hinged for the Dublin bridges and the deck crane jib laid flat along the cargo. Note the narrow-gauge brewery railway lines.

135 Fore-end of a Grand Canal motor boat, the 52 M, built in 1928. The stove chimney top was often fretted like an old locomotive's. Note too the carefully subdivided depth scales for tonnage calculations.

136

10 Tugs

Steam towage was a thankful innovation to inland navigation, particularly to rivers and lakes, where tides and currents made sailing and horse haulage exceptionally hazardous. A tug could, if powerful enough, force her way upstream with a long tow of barges which would have needed many men and horses to handle. Even the tug could be moderate in power if she could be designed to haul herself along by a cable laid in the bed of the river. This system was considered for several British navigations but never adopted, although widely applied in Europe.

On still canals tugs did not have quite the same attraction, because of the frequency of locks, which would have meant breaking up the tow. They were used, however, on long pounds, like the Wirral line of the Shropshire Union Canal, on the Birmingham system, and on the Bridgewater Canal. They had a particular value in tunnels and much ingenuity went into the design of specialist craft, like the electric tug at Harecastle Tunnel on the Trent and Mersey Canal, which did haul itself along by a cable laid in the tunnel invert, and like the self-centering tugs at Preston Brook (also on the Trent and Mersey) with their guide wheels.

As the illustrations will show, tugs came in all shapes and sizes, depending on the work they had to do, from large barge tugs on the Mersey to the little 'Bantam' pushers for handling spoil barges on the narrow canals.

Bridgewater Canal Tug
Steam powered screw tugs were introduced on the Bridgewater Canal in 1875 by that capable engineer, Edward Leader Williams. They followed an experiment with a cable hauling tug by John Fowler, of steam ploughing fame, and were very successful, eventually numbering twenty-five iron boats and one wooden. Some were built at Preston by Richard Smith, others at Stony Stratford on the Grand Junction by Edward Hayes. They were given local names like Stretford *and* Latchford *and towed three loaded flats on the Bridgewater Canal, although they could manage six on the deep wide waters of the Manchester Ship Canal. They measured up to 61ft long overall by 7ft 7in beam and had a horizontal single-cylinder engine exhausting to atmosphere, set parallel with the keel driving the screw through a bevel gear. The boiler was of locomotive type. They were fitted with diesel engines during the 1920s and a few survived until the 1960s. The hulls were built of long lasting wrought iron from the Low Moor Ironworks, Bradford.*

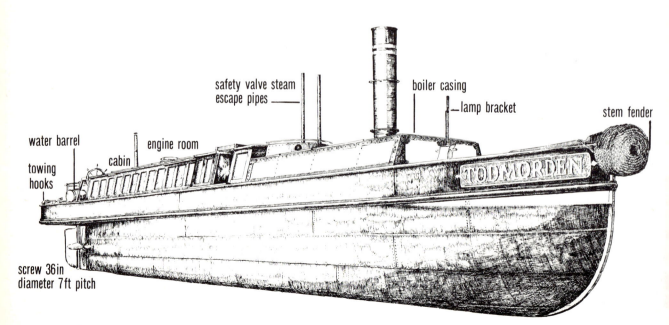

137 Generally called 'little packets' the Bridgewater Canal tugs were based at the top of Runcorn
Locks where they had their own dry dock, bunkers
and watering facilities. The packet in the foreground has just coaled up.

138 Coal traffic on the Aire and Calder Navigation and the Sheffield and South Yorkshire Navigation was handled within the limits of the navigations
by open holed barges, horse hauled or tug towed.
Some were in use until 1975 by the Leeds Co-
operative Society to bring coal to their Aireside
wharf near Leeds Station. They could carry up to
100 tons and were steel with a square stern. The
board secured to the after headledge of the hold
was simply a weather shield for the steerer. In this
1968 view the Leeds Co-op's tug *President* (sold in
1971) was towing a barge stern-first into Leeds
New Dock (opened in 1843) where the coal boats
lay before proceeding to the wharf.

139

139 Since the 1830s steam tugs had been in use on the Aire and Calder Navigation. The company themselves had a large number, many specially designed for the compartment boat traffic. This however is a barge tug passing under Leeds Bridge. Note the grips for pulling down the hinged funnel.

140 Steam towage came to the Thames above the tideway in the later nineteenth century after the formation of the Thames Conservancy in 1857, the new body assuming full jurisdiction in 1866. New locks were built and others modernized. This is a 1920s scene at Bell Weir lock above Staines, the barge being a tanker, one of the Thomas Clayton of Oldbury fleet, based at their Brentford depot. Like their well-known narrow boats, she bears a river name, *Medway*. She would measure some 70ft long by 13ft 6in beam, carrying up to 60 tons.

141 Islington Tunnel (960 yd and without a tow-path) on the Regent's Canal had a steam tug in attendance as early as 1826 — the first tunnel tug on a British canal, save for an earlier trial at Stand-edge on the Huddersfield Canal. The Islington tug hauled itself along by picking up a chain cable. The service lasted into the 1930s, the last tunnel tug being a motor one. By then tugs were handling a good deal of the traffic and a special one for tunnel work was superfluous. This is *Tring*, used for normal towing duties on the canal by British Waterways.

142 The Manchester Ship Canal was opened on 1 January 1894 and demanded a flotilla of tugs to handle the larger ships, particularly into the locks, where water resistance was such that a deep laden ship had to be forced in by two tugs, the bow one coming to the aid of the stern 'pusher.' The first MSC tugs were paddlers, the last paddle tug the *MSC Rixton* being withdrawn in 1955, and the last steam screw tugs the MSC *Bison* and *Badger* in 1966. Here *MSC Archer* is seen passing the Knutsford Road swing bridge, Warrington, on her way up the canal; she was built, like so many of the company's tugs, by Henry Robb of Leith in 1938 and was withdrawn in 1965.

142

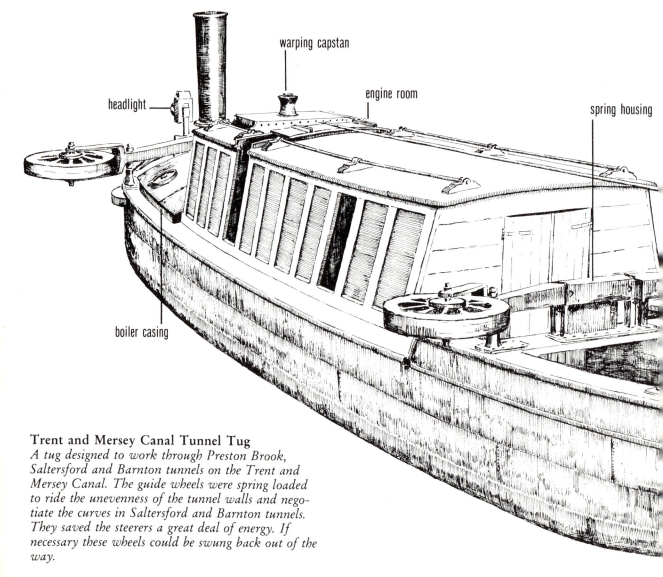

Trent and Mersey Canal Tunnel Tug

A tug designed to work through Preston Brook, Saltersford and Barnton tunnels on the Trent and Mersey Canal. The guide wheels were spring loaded to ride the unevenness of the tunnel walls and negotiate the curves in Saltersford and Barnton tunnels. They saved the steerers a great deal of energy. If necessary these wheels could be swung back out of the way.

143 Preston Brook Tunnel (1,239yd) on the Trent and Mersey Canal was the first major canal tunnel to be opened in the British Isles, in February 1775. There was no towpath and craft were legged or shafted through, until in 1864 a steam tug service was started. Four air shafts had to be sunk quickly and were opened in 1865, but not before a bricklayer had been overcome by fumes and drowned. The tugs were given spring-loaded guide wheels which rubbed along the side walls and saved steering. They maintained a 50-minute service backwards and forwards from 6.00am to 8.30pm until about 1943 when few horse boats were left. This tug is at the northern, Preston Brook end. Another tug worked the Saltersford and Barnton tunnels and one was in reserve.

144 and 145 Electric propulsion seemed to have a great future in the early 1900s; it was tried on the Wey Navigation at the turn of the century and later, in 1923, on the Staffordshire and Worcestershire Canal, current being picked up from overhead wires by a tramcar-type trolley pole. But although efficient, costs of wiring were high and the only long lasting installation was through Harecastle Tunnel on the Trent and Mersey Canal where an electric tug hauling itself along by a cable laid on the bottom was the only solution to ventilation problems. It was first installed in 1914, powered by batteries carried in an attendant boat, a second battery boat being on charge. But after World War I overhead wires were erected, the tug lasting until 1954 when powerful extractor fans were installed. These two scenes show: *top* the tug at the Chatterley end with its battery boat *below* the overhead wiring at the Chatterley end in 1953.

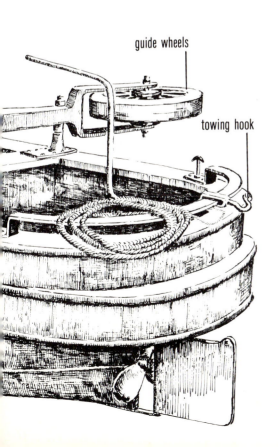

146

147

146 Steam and motor tugs never fully replaced horses on the Birmingham Canal Navigations where, because of all the many locks, mechanical power was no faster. The first motor tugs came in 1919, *Stentor* and *Hector* built by Walker's of Rickmansworth for Chance and Hunt, the Oldbury chemicals manufacturers, who already had steam tugs. Most Birmingham Canal Navigations motor tugs were about 40ft long with an engine of up to 36hp. Four loaded boats was an average tow, six was supposed to be the maximum, 800ft long and totalling 220 tons. This is *Stentor* just completed at Rickmansworth.

147 Motor tugs were less used on other narrow canals than the Birmingham system but were popular on river navigations, for example the Lee, the Trent, and the Severn. The London, Midland and Scottish Railway built some for maintenance work on the narrow Trent and Mersey Canal which they acquired at the railway grouping in 1923 as a legacy from the North Staffordshire Railway. This was one of a pair built by Yarwood's of Northwich in 1946, 25ft long with 18bhp engines, and wheel steering.

148 The Midland and Coast Canal Carrying Company took over some of the services and boats of the Shropshire Union Canal Company when the latter ceased to carry in 1921, and because of the long straight pounds of the Shropshire Union Canal main line and the regularly spaced locks in each flight, they tried towage of boats in trains by the motor tug *Energy*. She was fitted with a windlass so that she could bowhaul boats through the locks and a special shrouded propeller which would, because of the casing round the blades, concentrate the flow of water past the rudder, giving increased manoeuvrability. The scene is the former Shropshire Union dry dock at Chester.

11 Boats in Trains

The coupling of a string of small craft in a train is an old idea with modern applications, and gave great flexibility of operation. Large quantities of cargo could be passed through a small canal with restrictive lock dimensions. Moreover the train could be handled by a single power unit, a horse or a tug, and the crew could be cut to the minimum, for steerage could be achieved by various ingenious devices, from the guidance of a train of Shropshire Canal tub-boats by a man on the bank with a shaft, to the system of wires and buffers used on the Aire and Calder Navigation compartment boats.

Small craft had the advantage of easy handling, up and down inclined planes, and, at Goole, could be unloaded bodily in the port's coal hoists. The trains of little tub-boats in industrial East Shropshire have given place to 170-ton compartment boats in Yorkshire and the several methods of transporting push-tow barges aboard ocean going ships.

149

149 The tub-boat was of great industrial importance in East Shropshire, and it did much of the bulk mineral carrying in the Coalbrookdale-Wellington-Oakengates mining and ironmaking district (now Telford) before the railways came. The canals here, the Donnington Wood, the Wombridge, the Shropshire, the Ketley and the Shrewsbury, were designed for tub-boats, overcoming the plentiful changes of level by inclined planes as well as locks because water was short. Only small craft were possible on this type of canal, and tub-boats had the advantage of flexibility. They could be made up into trains as the trade required, with as many as twenty boats being pulled behind a single horse with one man in charge, driving the horse and steering the train with a shaft from the bank. Capacities per boat varied from 8 tons on the Ketley Canal to 5 tons on the Shropshire and Shrewsbury Canals.

Shropshire Canal Tub Boats
A train of Shropshire Canal tub-boats, the ancestors of the Aire and Calder Navigation compartment boats. A single horse could manage a train of twenty guided by a shaft from the bank, wielded by the horse driver.

train of up to twenty boats

steering shaft

pad for shaft point   timber head

Tug and Train of Compartment Boats

Aire and Calder Navigation tug and train of nineteen compartment boats; this became the standard number between Castleford and Goole, because the locks could take the tug and train in one penning.

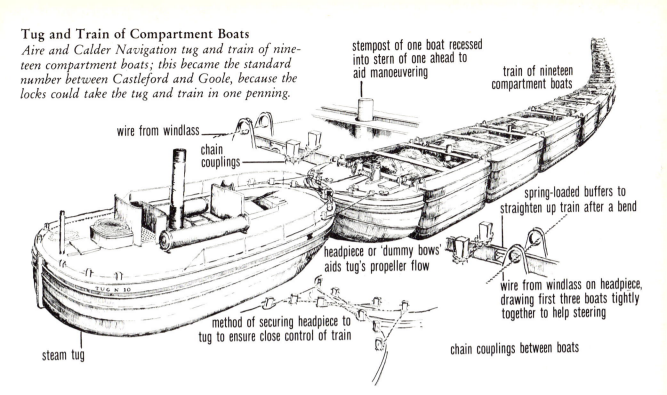

wire from windlass

chain couplings

stempost of one boat recessed into stern of one ahead to aid manoeuvering

train of nineteen compartment boats

spring-loaded buffers to straighten up train after a bend

headpiece or 'dummy bows' aids tug's propeller flow

wire from windlass on headpiece, drawing first three boats tightly together to help steering

method of securing headpiece to tug to ensure close control of train

chain couplings between boats

steam tug

150 Coal has been a staple cargo on the Aire and Calder Navigation since the eighteenth century, but a really cheap method of carrying it down to Goole for export was not evolved until W.H. Bartholomew's patent of 1862 for compartment boats, which were enlarged tub-boats, to be pushed in trains of six by a steam tug. They were in service from 1865, each boat having a capacity of 35 tons, measuring 21ft long by 15ft wide by 8ft deep and drawing 6ft 6in laden. Pushing was successful, but the trade demanded larger trains than the tugs could manage and from the 1900s compartment boats were pulled, up to forty at a time. The 'dummy bows' of the push tows were retained to safeguard the tug's propeller flow. By the opening of the New Junction Canal in 1905 compartment boats — 'pans', 'Bartholomew's bread pans' or 'Tom Puddings' — were extended to the Sheffield and South Yorkshire Navigation. This is a 1936 scene near Doncaster.

150

151

151 At St John's Colliery, Normanton in South Yorkshire, the 35-ton compartment boats were loaded a mile and a half from the Wakefield line of the Aire and Calder Navigation at Stanley Ferry. A railway carried them to Newlands Basin where the special twelve-wheel wagon descended into the water, braked by the locomotive at the end of a wire rope passing round a snatch block. The locomotive could only manage one compartment boat at a time. Note the spring-loaded buffers on the boat which straightened up the train after bends. The colliery railway closed in about 1941.

152 35-ton compartment boats have been eclipsed by the 170-ton capacity craft serving Ferrybridge C Power Station, introduced in 1965. Loaded trains of three or more are pushed by a diesel tug with an inboard-outboard drive which allows extraordinary manoeuvrability. After unloading at the Ferrybridge tippler the tug can turn her propeller unit 180° to head her train of empties back to the colliery staith. Here a train is on its way from Parkhill Colliery, Wakefield.

153 In this picture we see the method of securing a modern pusher tug to her train of large capacity compartment boats. The two wire hawsers are passed round bollards and the slack taken up by a couple of screw-threaded tensioners, while the two pushing knees fit into recesses in the stern of the compartment boat.

152

153

154

154 The Ferrybridge C Power Station tippler which handles the 170-ton coal compartment boats. A travelling boom, called a 'Jumbo', pushes the boats into position and the hoist lifts, tips and lowers each compartment boat in nine minutes. Sixty boats a day are dealt with, which means 51,000 tons of coal a week.

155 Push towing has been advanced from the coal trade to general merchandise, and for that matter to spoil boats taking away dredgings. It has the advantage of giving the tug complete control over the tow, which in effect becomes a self-propelled barge, the tug providing motive power and steerage so that helmsmen on the tow are not needed. Push-tow barges are being designed for carriage in a ship, hence their rectangular shape for ease of stowage. From March 1974 to December 1975 a ship called

BACAT 1 ran between the Humber, the Tees and Rotterdam. BACAT stands for 'barge aboard catamaran', and the twin-hulled vessel owned in Denmark could carry ten 140-ton barges and three 370-ton. From Hull where the ship berthed, the 140-ton craft were pushed up the Aire and Calder Navigation, the River Ouse to Selby, the Sheffield and South Yorkshire Navigation to Rotherham and the River Trent. Dock labour disputes precluded further use of this service.

156 BACAT barges at the British Waterways Board depot at Rotherham, on the Sheffield and South Yorkshire Navigation, with one of the BWB pusher tugs which brought them up from the Humber. They and their parent ship were registered at Rudkøbing in Denmark.

155

156

12 Passenger Packets

Passenger services were pretty widespread on the navigations of the British Isles, particularly in Scotland and Ireland. Early packets were not particularly refined in design, being fairly beamy craft with a long cabin amidships, possibly divided into two classes with a galley or steward's pantry amidships, and some open deck space fore and aft. For river work they had to be generously wide, but the still water of a canal allowed scope for advances in naval architecture. The advances came from Scotland with extensive trials in 1830 on the Paisley and the Forth and Clyde Canals, and the result was the swift boat, very slender and shallow draughted. Pulled by two horses, the lightly-built hull could plane and speeds of 10mph were achieved. Several English canals and the Grand Canal in Ireland bought swift boats and they provided efficient and reliable services, competing successfully with the stage

coaches and on the Lancaster with the trains.

But locomotive speeds soon forced swift boats out of business and except in special circumstances powered passenger craft hardly caught on. The special circumstances were mainly on the larger rivers, notably in Yorkshire and in Scotland and Ireland. Steam packets preceded railways in Yorkshire and remained in service until World War I, albeit much reduced by railway competition. In Scotland steamers had long careers on the Caledonian, the Crinan and the Forth and Clyde Canals, as they did on the River Shannon and its lakes. Nowadays passenger services have revived in the shape of the day excursion boat which is widespread over the canal system, and the hotel and self-drive hire cruiser. But these are not regular passenger links, which have completely gone.

157　Scottish swift passenger boats were introduced on the Lancaster Canal in 1833, cutting the Preston-Kendal schedules to eight hours and the Preston-Lancaster to three. Eventually there were four, 72ft long by 6ft wide by 2ft 6½in deep, this maximum depth being at the forefoot. The last, *Crewdson* (illustrated) became an inspection boat with the name *Waterwitch II* and was intact until World War II. Ninety passengers were carried in

two classes, first forward, second aft with the bar amidships. The seats were arranged along the cabin sides and people sat facing inwards. They could see out but the windows were small, so in fine weather many must have gone out into the wells fore and aft. Here *Waterwitch II* is at the Lancaster boathouse, before the cabin was shortened as later photographs show.

157

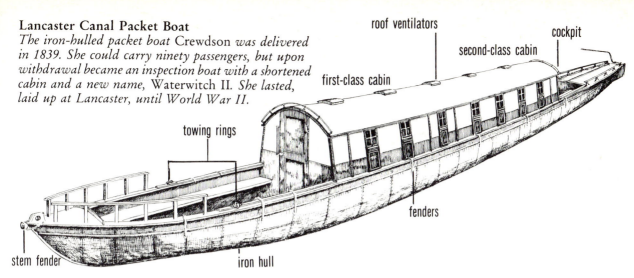

Lancaster Canal Packet Boat

The iron-hulled packet boat Crewdson *was delivered in 1839. She could carry ninety passengers, but upon withdrawal became an inspection boat with a shortened cabin and a new name,* Waterwitch II. *She lasted, laid up at Lancaster, until World War II.*

roof ventilators

cockpit

second-class cabin

first-class cabin

towing rings

fenders

stem fender

iron hull

158

158 Photographs of canal passenger craft in service are rare, since most went out of business with the arrival of the railways, before the camera could record them. An exception was the boat used on the Ancholme Navigation in Lincolnshire which lasted until about 1905. She was the *Gem* which ran between Ferriby Sluice and Brigg, meeting the Hull steam packet at Ferriby Sluice. This picture shows a mid-1890s scene at Ferriby Sluice. Two horses hauled *Gem* and the crew comprised captain, steward and horseman.

159 Irish Grand Canal passenger services started in 1780 before the line was complete and speeded up during the 1800s when night and day fly-boats were introduced to the loss of the canal company's chain of hotels. *Pomeroy* was one of these, named after the two Pomeroys, Arthur who became Lord Harberton and his son the Hon & Rev J. Pomeroy, both committeemen of the Grand Canal. She was built in 1807 and had, as the model shows, a first-class cabin forward, a second-class aft, a bar and both ladies' and gentlemen's lavatory accommodation amidships. She was sold in 1834 when Scottish swift boats were introduced; but a second *Pomeroy* followed, a light wooden boat for local services in Dublin. The model is in the collection of the Old Dublin Society.

160

161

160 *Caledonia* was a passenger paddle steamer, in service on the Trent in 1814 between Hull and Gainsborough, and in 1817 steamers ran between Nottingham and Gainsborough. Packet services lasted until about 1914 between Hull and Gainsborough and this view of the Packet Landing at Gainsborough shows left to right, *Scarborough* built in 1866, *Atalanta* built in 1851, and *Isle of Axholme* built in 1860, the last two owned by the Gainsborough United Steam Packet Company.

161 Hull Corporation Pier with two of the Goole and Hull Steam Packet Company passenger steamers: to the left *Empress* on the Goole service, to the right *Her Majesty* which ran to Ferriby Sluice. *Empress* was built in 1893 and *Her Majesty* in 1860. Neither steamer service survived World War I.

162 Canal passenger services were at their most efficient in Scotland after the introduction of swift boats in the 1830s, following trials on the Glasgow, Paisley and Johnstone Canal and on the Forth and Clyde Canal. From Paisley to Glasgow only took 45 minutes, the boats averaging 10mph behind two horses. Several boats were sold to England (eg to the Lancaster Canal) and more followed when railways started to compete from the 1840s. On the Forth and Clyde Canal inter-city passenger services ceased by 1848, but shorter services stayed and much later there were pleasure steamers, notably the 'Queen' fleet of James Aitken and Company Ltd of Kirkintilloch. Their *Fairy Queen* (illustrated) of 1897 was their second, here seen on the summit level at Craigmarloch near Kilsyth whence they ran to Kirkintilloch.

163

164

163 One of the pioneers of the Caledonian Canal passenger service, here seen at Fort Augustus, was *Edinburgh Castle* built in 1844 for service in the Clyde but transferred to the Caledonian Canal in 1846. Various operators had her, ending with David MacBrayne, who gave her an extensive re-fit in 1875 and a new name more suitable to Inverness-shire, *Glengarry.* She lasted in service, paired with *Gondolier,* until she was broken up in 1927. She was powered by an interesting single-cylinder steeple engine.

164 In 1866 David MacBrayne's added to their West Highland passenger and mail steamer services by commissioning *Gondolier* to run the length of the Caledonian Canal between Banavie (above the eight staircase locks), Fort Augustus and Inverness. She was built by J. & G. Thomson, Clydebank, and was 148.2ft long with compound engines. She remained in service until 1939.

165 Passengers aboard the *Gondolier* look down on a fishing vessel following them through the Caledonian Canal. She is a Banff boat, almost certainly a 'zulu', a type of sailing drifter first built in 1878, the time of the Zulu Wars. Moray Firth fishermen were and are important users of the canal as they pursue the migrations of the herring. The picture is from a hand coloured slide dated 1911.

Steam Packet Station

166

167

166 Steam passenger services on the River Shannon were started in 1826 with the *Marquis Wellesley*, but a much larger iron vessel was delivered in 1833, *Lady Lansdowne*, which ran on Lough Derg, being too big to leave it, for she measured 133ft by 17ft by 9ft 6in deep. She was left to decay when services were given up in 1862 on the arrival of the railway, and her remains lie at Killaloe. She had an 80ft consort, *Burgoyne*, which ran from Killaloe up to Athlone. The illustration is a detail from William Stokes' *Pictorial Survey and Tourists' Guide to Lough Derg and the River Shannon* (1842) and shows the large diameter paddle wheels of the *Lady Lansdowne*. Astern of her lie a couple of luggage boats which were towed by the steamers.

167 Passenger services on the River Shannon and the lakes were briefly revived in 1897 by the Shannon Development Company. They put on a daily weekday summer service from Killaloe to Athlone and to Dromod on Lough Bofin, with a twice-weekly winter schedule. They had six vessels, three of them large ones with room for 200 passengers, including the *Countess of Cadogan* here seen approaching Portumna at the head of Lough Derg. She remained with them until 1913 when she went to Lough Corrib. All Shannon passenger services ceased in 1914, by then reduced to a summer daily trip each way between Killaloe and Banagher, indeed there had been no regular year-round sailings since 1903.

13 Ferries

Most ferries cross rivers and are or were of many types: rope or chain worked, dependent on sweeps, on the motion of the current, and on steam or internal combustion engines. Some were specially designed to ferry boat horses across to the other path, others could carry vehicles. Canal ferries are rare but houses on the offside bank often have a boat to get across to the towpath side.

168   Ferries were a feature of the Upper Thames, not only where the towpath changed sides as at Sandford below Iffley, but to provide a public service. This one is illustrated by H.R. Robertson in his pleasantly readable *Life on the Upper Thames*, published in 1875. The ferry was pulled across hand-over-hand by a rope passing between two vertical rollers on the gunwhale, the rope being tensioned by a windlass on the bank.

168

169   A rope-worked ferry on the River Severn below Welsh Bridge, Shrewsbury, operated in exactly the same way as the Thames one illustrated by H.R. Robertson.

169

170

170 Because of frequent floods and a strong current the Severn was a difficult river to bridge and ferries were common. On the narrow upper reaches some of them depended on the stream for movement, swinging across at the end of a rope made fast to the bank like a pendulum. The rope passed through a pulley at the masthead and down to the deck so that it could be adjusted to match the water level. The rudder was extra large for manoeuvring. This is the Coalport ferry, large enough (as was the one at Ironbridge) to take horses and carts. The white at the stem would indicate the boat's position at night. The last one in use, up to 1972, was the foot passenger ferry at Arley near Bewdley.

14 Maintenance Craft

River and canal maintenance demands a wide variety of vessels. They range in size from ladder bucket dredgers to small pontoons or flats for transporting hedge trimmings. Dredgers come in many varieties and much thought is given to their design, the great need on canals being accuracy of positioning, to deal with silt accumulated against lock gates and rubbish in bridge holes. Humdrum but necessary are the mud boats to carry away the spoil. This could rarely be dropped through bottom doors due to lack of depth, but had to be dug out, more laborious than filling.

Ice paralyses a canal very quickly unless efficient ice-breakers are available. The problem is to break a channel wide enough to allow boats a clear passage. On the smaller canals this was done by rocking the ice breaker, but larger canals and rivers (although the latter were not so prone to ice) demanded bigger ice breakers.

Engineering work needed a great number of craft. Boats to carry bricks, sand, cement, tools; boats to carry pumps to clear lock chambers and bridge holes; boats to carry a blacksmith's forge, a pile-driving rig, electric-generating equipment, air compressors; boats to mount staging for the inspection of tunnel linings. Then there were inspection launches for the engineers and often elaborate committee boats, the directors' saloons of the navigation companies. Some companies could not afford their own, and as they were so rarely used a boat would be hired or converted for the annual inspection.

171

171 Narrow canal authorities for long depended on the primitive but effective spoon dredger, which was slow but able to tackle awkward corners. Eventually the Priestman patent grab and its modifications replaced the man-handled spoon, but it lasted on some waterways into the 1950s. On the Trent and Mersey Canal the North Staffordshire Railway Company, the canal's owners, had *Oregon*. One man guides the spoon, another works the crane, and a third attends the windlass to pull the spoon into the mud. This dredger seems to carry her own spoil, the spoon being pierced with holes to drain off the water.

172

173

172 A Priestman grab dredger working on the Monmouthshire Canal sometime before 1915. The Priestman brothers of Hull took out their first grab patent in 1877 and built up a world market for their invention. For canal dredging the grab had the advantage of being able to reach awkward corners. This was one of four supplied to the Great Western Railway, the 8ft 6in wide pontoon using timber side floats to increase stability when working. The pontoon was manoeuvered by wires to windlasses fore and aft.

173 A small Priestman grab on the Suffolk Stour, with the crane and boiler mounted low down to pass under bridges. There are floats at each side to increase stability. The picture comes from a Priestman catalogue of 1915.

174 Another Priestman catalogue picture of the Manchester Ship Canal dredger *Beta* built in 1891. This vessel had a 58 cu ft grab and filled her own 300-ton capacity hopper in $2\frac{1}{4}$ hours. She would then proceed down the canal to the sea to empty her spoil through bottom doors.

175 Hard at work on the restoration of the Basingstoke Canal is an ex-Grand Union grab dredger built in 1934. She was built by Grafton and Company of Bedford who delivered their first to the Grand Junction Canal in 1896. The Grafton dredger was designed to place the grab with great accuracy, an advantage in canal work. This precision was made possible by the boom which carried the grab, raised and lowered and slewed by the crane. The grab itself was mounted at the foot of a rigid frame and was opened and shut by a special cylinder, receiving steam via its pivots in the boom framework. Many canal companies were using the Grafton steam dredger up to the 1960s, but this is the only working survivor. Side pontoons give extra stability.

Grafton Steam Grab Dredger
A steam dredger currently working on the restoration of the Basingstoke Canal but supplied new to the Grand Union Canal Company in 1934.

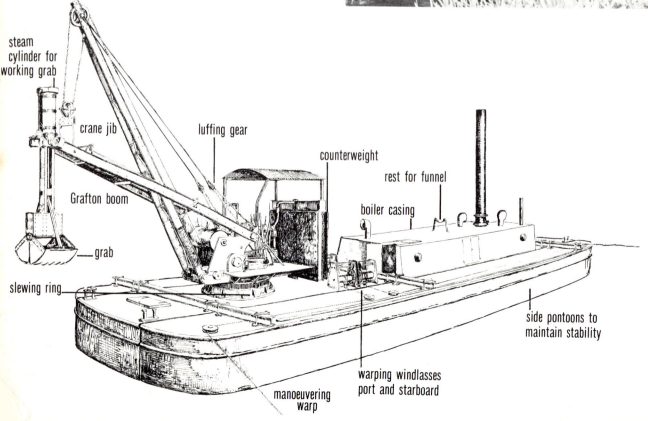

steam cylinder for working grab

crane jib

luffing gear

counterweight

rest for funnel

boiler casing

Grafton boom

grab

slewing ring

side pontoons to maintain stability

manoeuvering warp

warping windlasses port and starboard

176

176 A bow-well ladder-bucket dredger on the Mersey at Warrington in the 1950s. The buckets are linked in an endless chain, travelling round tumbler wheels at each end of a long boom. This is hinged at the inner end, the outer projecting beyond the dredger's hull and raised and lowered by a powerful hoist at the bow. The buckets travel up the boom and tip into chutes at the top, whence the spoil passes into barges. The buckets have a sharp cutting face which bites into the river bed. Many bucket dredgers are non self-propelled and put out mooring wires which they adjust to follow a precise pattern of work. These craft are mainly used in rivers and harbours, and there is one for example on the River Weaver.

177 Dredgers need a constant procession of spoil boats to remove the muck; at least three have to be in attendance, one loading from the dredger, one unloading at the dumping ground and one or better two in transit. Few spoil or mud boats are self propelled, but the Weaver Navigation had three steam ones with rounded bows, *Whale, Shark* and *Grampus*, one of which (*Whale*) once went to Belfast to help in the deepening of the Lagan Navigation. Although often called mud hoppers, these craft rarely had bottom-opening doors, because there was never sufficient depth on the dumping grounds to use them. Here in February 1922 the much travelled *Whale* attends bucket dredger No 3, built in 1867.

178 Ice-breaking was a necessity to keep canal traffic and (in severe conditions) river traffic moving. As wide a channel as possible was needed, so smaller ice boats were rocked from side to side by men grasping a central rail. On wider navigations in more recent times tugs were, and indeed are, used but some narrow canal ice-breakers remained horse drawn into the 1950s, for example on the Birmingham Canal Navigations. Possibly the first iron-hulled ice breaker was delivered to the Ashby Canal in 1808, and iron was understandably popular, wooden hulls having to be sheathed with plates. This is an iron Shropshire Union example with a demonstration crew aboard. Note the inverted hook for the towline, or lines, as several horses might be in use.

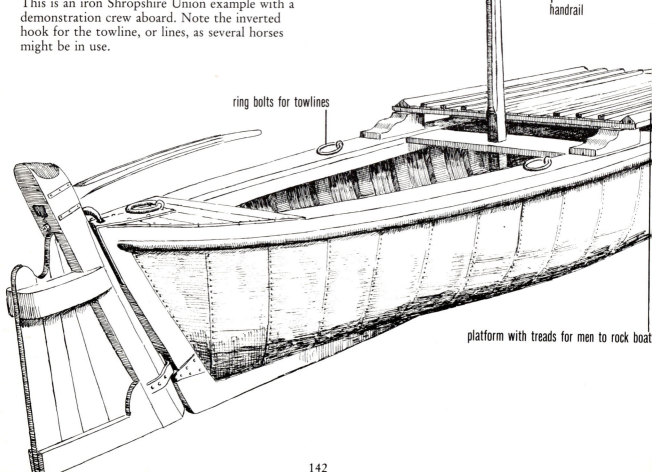

handrail

ring bolts for towlines

platform with treads for men to rock boat

179 Larger waterways demanded more than the man-rocked ice-breaker, and the Crinan Canal in Argyllshire had a purpose built steamer called *Conway*, built in 1894 and broken up in 1964. She was built by Napier, Shanks and Bell on the Clyde and had, as can be seen, a bluff spoon-shaped stem which would ride up on the ice and smash it by the weight of the hull. Here is a view of the vessel on the shore at Ardrishaig awaiting her end.

180 Preserved and famous, here is the Staffordshire and Worcestershire Canal's committee boat *Lady Hatherton*, built in 1896, and named after the chairman's wife. She stayed with the company until nationalization and British Waterways used her for inspection tours. Now a pleasure boat, she has had a new hull modelled on the old one, but the cabin is original, complete with plush upholstery and the canal company's monogram etched in the windows.

181 In 1878 the Leeds and Liverpool Canal commissioned a steam committee boat called *Water Witch* (such a common name on the canals). A second *Water Witch* (illustrated) followed in 1915, built by the canal company at their Wigan yard. She was 61ft long and remained in service until 1951. She had a special mooring basin at Wigan, by the twenty-third lock.

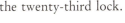
wooden planked hull sheathed in ice plates

Narrow Canal Ice-Breaker
A standard design of wooden-hulled narrow canal ice-breaker, of well-rounded cross section, longitudinally planked throughout. The men stood on the platform to rock the boat and break as wide a channel through the ice as possible.

Index

Numbers in italics refer to illustrations.